MW00799476

PRAISE FOR *TRINITY AND CREATION*

"We live in a day when Christians tend to think of God as merely a bigger version of themselves. As a result, the Creator is not distinguished from the creature, and key attributes or perfections are either abandoned or significantly modified. Barcellos has issued a much-needed wake-up call, one that rightly distinguishes the Creator from the creature, refusing to compromise the Creator's simplicity, immutability, timeless eternality, aseity, and much more. Contrary to popular assumptions, apart from this classical view of God, creation itself has no adequate explanation. Every serious student of theology should read Barcellos and return to these ancient paths. Only then will we avoid the temptation that modern theology has fallen into, that is, the temptation to domesticate God."

—Matthew Barrett, author of *None Greater: The Undomesticated Attributes of God*

"Richard Barcellos offers a meticulous analysis of the Second London Confession of Faith's treatment of the doctrine of creation, carefully explaining how the concise statement unfolds into a robust and trinitarian systematic theology of creation. Along the way he is able to clearly identify the contours of historic Reformed orthodoxy on the doctrine of creation while identifying deviations from this tradition among certain contemporary Reformed evangelicals. The theological options are clearly outlined, and Barcellos makes a compelling case for historic orthodoxy, leaving no doubt as to the dogmatic issues at stake. This work will have considerable pedagogical and catechetical value in Reformed contexts."

—Glenn Butner, author of *The Son Who Learned Obedience: A Theological Case Against the Eternal Submission of the Son*

"So much contemporary theology betrays a dangerous impatience with mystery and the limitations of creaturely knowledge of God. In a vain attempt to bring God into a closer relationship to creation, even some Reformed and evangelical theologians now are denying God's simplicity and immutability. They seem to think that they can change classical, Nicene, metaphysical doctrines, yet still somehow escape the pitfalls those doctrines were designed to avoid. But to say that God is both changing and unchanging is not a paradox, but a contradiction, and by introducing contradictions into our doctrine of God they destabilize it in dangerous ways. In this careful work, Richard Barcellos patiently explains, in a step-by-step way, the reasons why the metaphysical doctrines of classical theism are enshrined within the Reformed creeds of the seventeenth century and why it is folly to abandon this creedal wisdom for contemporary fads. This is an enlightening and clearly argued book, which contributes to the retrieval of classical orthodoxy in our day."

—Craig A. Carter, author of *Interpreting Scripture with the Great Tradition: Recovering the Genius of Premodern Exegesis*

"*Trinity and Creation: A Scriptural and Confessional Account* is a stunningly rich and marvelously astute study of the Creator/creature distinction, one often lost in our theological talk today. Richard Barcellos has served the church of Christ well and has given us a delightful example of theological writing that makes the spirit praise, the mind expand, and the heart soar."

—Liam Goligher, Tenth Presbyterian Church, Philadelphia, Pennsylvania

"Richard Barcellos writes with insight and great economy setting out the trinitarian doctrine of creation, embodying in this account the general hermeneutical insights of Scripture that it implies.... This doctrine of the creation expresses the purest trinitarian theism, in understanding that God—infinite, eternal, unchangeable—creates *ex nihilo* a finite universe of time and space, and subject to change. The unchanging God gives being to a creation that is teeming with change.... This study is both demanding and uplifting. It is highly recommended."

—Paul Helm, King's College, London

"Understanding the doctrines of God and creation, and the relationship between them, is the lifeblood of systematic theology. Richard Barcellos shows ably how and why the triune God remains unchanged by creation even while all things in creation relate to him. The result is a piece of sound confessional theology that addresses contemporary controversies fairly and biblically, while placing the doctrine of the Trinity at the center of the doctrine of creation."

—Ryan M. McGraw, Greenville Presbyterian Theological Seminary

"The biblical proclamation of creation is first and foremost a revelation of the eternal, unchangeable, almighty, sovereign, transcendent, immanent, trinitarian God. Christ's church has borne witness to this God-glorifying theology of creation from the beginning. Rooted in Scripture, faithful to confessional orthodoxy, supplemented from major theological writings, and juxtaposed with modern aberrant proposals, Dr. Barcellos's book guides the reader sure-footedly along the way of truth about God the Creator. It is time to address these fundamental aspects of the doctrine of creation long neglected in the battle over evolution. Creation should be an occasion of knowing and praising God before rushing to apologetics. I recommend this clarion call to embrace the architectonic doctrine of God."

—D. Scott Meadows, Calvary Baptist Church (Reformed), Exeter, New Hampshire

Trinity and Creation

Trinity and Creation

A Scriptural and Confessional Account

RICHARD C. BARCELLOS

RESOURCE *Publications* · Eugene, Oregon

TRINITY AND CREATION
A Scriptural and Confessional Account

Resource Publications
An Imprint of Wipf and Stock Publishers
199 W. 8th Ave., Suite 3
Eugene, OR 97401

www.wipfandstock.com

PAPERBACK ISBN: 978-1-7252-8034-2
HARDCOVER ISBN: 978-1-7252-8038-0
EBOOK ISBN: 978-1-7252-8040-3

Contents

Preface

THE SUBSTANCE OF THIS book began as lectures, delivered at the Southern California Reformed Baptist Pastors' Conference 2017, La Mirada, CA. I thank the board for entrusting me with the stewardship of addressing the vast subject of creation according to the confession of faith. When first assigned the topic, I was not aware of just how deep and richly theological the subject was. Now I know better. I am thankful for various editorial readers for helping make the final product more palatable. I am very thankful for my church, Grace Reformed Baptist Church, Palmdale, CA, which encourages me in my various writing projects. My dear wife, Nan, always supports me and puts up with my late nights, early mornings, and reading out loud to her while driving during crunch time. Thanks, honey!

Though this book has been written primarily for pastors and theological students, studious Christians should be able to profit from its contents. Though it focuses on seventeenth-century British confessions of faith, all serious-minded Christians of various denominations should profit from its content, especially since I ground confessional formulations in Holy Scripture itself.

I want to express special thanks to two friends. J. V. Fesko's many books and private discussions have taught me how to go about retrieving old truths for new days. His tireless labors for the advancement of the old paths has both challenged and encouraged me to put my hand to the plow and not look back. James M. Renihan, my teaching colleague, has taught me by his life, writings, and lectures on the confession of faith how to do Christian theology in a Christian manner. Though I have a long way to go on many fronts, these two men have helped me tremendously. Thank you, brothers.

I will be citing the Westminster Confession of Faith and the Second London Confession of Faith. When the Westminster Confession is cited it comes from *Westminster Confession of Faith,* published by Free Presbyterian Publications, fifth reprint, 1988. The Second London Confession is cited from *A Confession of Faith, 1677,* published by B&R Press, facsimile edition, 2000.

May the Lord be pleased to use this work for his glory and the good of many souls. *Soli Deo gloria*!

RICHARD C. BARCELLOS, PH.D.
Pastor of Grace Reformed Baptist Church
Palmdale, CA
Associate Professor of Exegetical Theology
IRBS Theological Seminary
Mansfield, TX
July 2020

1

Introduction

IT MAY BE HELPFUL to explain the title and sub-title of this book. By "Trinity and Creation" is meant the triune God and everything not God. Another way of putting it is "God plus the world." As will be argued below, older theologians understood "the world" in the context of discussing God and creation to mean everything created, or creatures. The words "A Scriptural and Confessional Account" encapsulate the fact that the arguments will be grounded in the Scriptures, utilizing the doctrinal formulations of the Westminster Confession of Faith 1646 (WCF), the Savoy Declaration 1658 (SD), and the Second London Confession of Faith 1677/89 (2LCF), which declare the Father, Son, and Holy Spirit as co-equal, divine agents of creation. The confession will be used to provide an outline for the study.[1] The book not only states the confessional doctrine of trinitarian creation but seeks to account for its formulation. The word "confessional" refers to the three seventeenth-century documents mentioned above, though other creedal documents will be consulted at various points. Accounting for the confessional formulation of trinitarian creation will bring us into a discussion of hermeneutics and theological method. It is one thing to state and explain a confessional formulation; it is another to account for it. Though hermeneutics and theological method, when it comes to accounting for the

1. I will be working off of the 2LCF because it is what I confess.

confession's statement on creation, are a large part of this book, it will adhere closely to the doctrine of the Trinity as well. This will be largely assumed throughout the discussion. The reason for this is due to the fact that chapter 4 of the confession, "Of Creation" assumes chapters 1–3 (i.e., "Of the Holy Scriptures," "Of God and of the Holy Trinity," and "Of God's Decree").

This book attempts to present a method of accounting for the confessional formulation of the doctrine of creation by our triune God. Formulating Christian doctrine, especially as it relates to the doctrine of the Trinity, is not as simple as counting texts which use the same words; nor is it as simple as rehearsing redemptive history. Counting texts that use the same or synonymous words is deficient in establishing Christian doctrine. This is because biblical texts ought to be weighed, not merely counted, to determine their importance. This will be illustrated in various parts of the book. Weighing texts is especially important when considering creation in relation to the Creator. If only one text of Holy Scripture informs us about a crucial element of the divine act of creation, that text is of great importance. One of the reasons this is the case is because creation involves *everything* in relation to God. The doctrine of creation, as with the doctrine of the Trinity, is a distributed doctrine. John Webster's words capture what is meant by creation and the doctrine of the Trinity as distributed doctrines. He says:

> . . . the doctrine of creation is one of the two distributed doctrines in the corpus of Christian dogmatics. The first (both in sequence and in material primacy) distributed doctrine is the doctrine of the Trinity, of which all other articles of Christian teaching are an amplification or application, and which therefore permeates theological affirmations about every matter; theology talks about everything by talking about God. The doctrine of creation is the second distributed doctrine, although, because its scope is restricted to the *opera Dei ad extra* [i.e., the external works of God], its distribution is less comprehensive than that of the doctrine of the Trinity. Within this limit, the doctrine of creation is ubiquitous. It is not restricted to one particular point in the sequence of Christian doctrine, but provides orientation and a measure of governance to all that theology has to say about all things in relation to God.[2]

Because both God the Trinity and creation are distributed doctrines, it is of the utmost importance that we allow the Bible to speak on these issues, even if it does not speak as often as it does on other issues. We do not need

---

2. John Webster, *God without Measure: Working Papers in Christian Theology, Volume I, God and the Works of God* (London, Oxford, New York, New Delhi, Sydney: Bloomsbury, 2016), 117.

a plethora of biblical texts indicating the work of the Spirit in creation, for example. One text would suffice, and its truth would extend to the entirety of Christian thinking on creation, conservation, re-creation, and consummation. Scriptural texts must be weighed not merely counted, especially as they relate to telling us something about God and his works.

Formulating Christian doctrine is also more involved than a rehearsal of redemptive history. Though the study of redemptive history (i.e., biblical theology) is a vital aspect of the theological encyclopedia, it concerns itself with the revelatory process presented to us in Holy Scripture. Its method is not designed to conclude its work by presenting full statements on the various *loci* (i.e., places) of systematic theology. Unlike biblical theology, systematic theology is designed to collate various aspects of revelation under pre-determined headings (e.g., Scripture, God, creation, providence, etc.).[3] When systematic theology does its work properly, each topic's statements are formulated by a canonical consultation, a consultation of Scripture as a finished product of divine revelation, and in conversation with historical theology. Systematic theology reduces all the truths of Holy Scripture concerning given topics to propositional form. Similarly, confessional formulations seek to reduce large swaths of biblical truth into brief compass. In order to do this successfully, these formulations must weigh texts in order to ensure the formulations are brief, though comprehensive, enough to accurately convey the major emphases of Holy Scripture. These points will be illustrated in the discussion below.

OVERVIEW OF THE BOOK

After the Introduction, chapter 2 seeks to put confession 4.1, mentioned above, in context. Once this is done, a discussion on hermeneutics and theological method, in light of the confession, will be conducted.

The third chapter covers most of the relevant issues of confession 4.1. Some issues are covered in more depth than others. The reason for this is due to the scope of this book.

Chapter 4 seeks to define creation. After providing a working definition of creation, a brief survey of seventeenth-century theologians on creation will be conducted. This sets up the fifth chapter.

Chapter 5 is a contemporary excursus. It analyzes some of John M. Frame's and K. Scott Oliphint's published material on God and creation

---

3. We must not think that these pre-determined headings come from outside of Holy Scripture, imposed upon it to make sense of it. The doctrinal places of systematic theology come about due to contemplation upon Scripture.

which, it will be argued, is not in-step with how older theologians stated themselves on these issues. Both Frame and Oliphint state clearly that they are uncomfortable with various aspects of older ways of accounting for the acts of God given creation. The views of these men were chosen due to their relation to the WCF and their influence through their published materials.[4]

Chapter 6 takes readers back to the doctrine of the Trinity and creation, focusing specifically on the doctrine of appropriations in John Owen's "Peculiar Works of the Holy Spirit in the First or Old Creation." Owen's work illustrates many of the points made in previous discussion about hermeneutics, theological method, and accounting for trinitarian creation.

The Conclusion is a brief recapitulation of the book with some suggestions on how its contents might help pastors and theological students.

THE TEXT OF CONFESSION 4.1

Confession 4.1 will be analyzed using the 2LCF as the basis, though other creedal documents will be cited. Since 2LCF is slightly different in form

---

4. It may interest some readers to know that in May of 2019 I corresponded with K. Scott Oliphint concerning some of his views addressed in chapter 5 of this book, as well as the Appendix. Dr. Oliphint was kind enough to respond to my request that he preview my material where I critique some of his published statements. Though I remain unpersuaded by all of his explanations of those published statements and their entailments, I have revised some of my material in light of our correspondence and have sought to represent his views fairly. Interested readers are encouraged to read *all* the footnotes which address aspects of Dr. Oliphint's views in chapter 5. Also, I am aware that a joint statement by Westminster Theological Seminary and Dr. Oliphint was posted at the Westminster Theological Seminary website on June 22, 2020. The statement includes these words: "Given the controversy surrounding *God With Us*, Dr. Oliphint determined, for the good and peace of the church (Rom. 12:18), to repudiate his proposals concerning the essential/covenantal classification of God's characteristics, as well as their implications for the incarnation. Dr. Oliphint no longer believes these proposals to be helpful or worth pursuing, and will no longer write, speak or teach them." The final sentence of the joint statement reads as follows: "Dr. Oliphint's proposals concerning the essential/covenantal classification of God's attributes, as well as their implications for the incarnation, wherever they exist in any of his writings or lectures heretofore, should be interpreted in view of this statement." Available at https://www.wts.edu/wp-content/uploads/2020/06/Statement-June-22-2020.pdf?mc_cid=68b47306ca&mc_eid=eac21fa36a&fbclid=IwAR1SqVmBUtjeKLERoP-R9EU8Ug0434Ng1AIUI1aG9XiWiyG9Xc1mMg00PIk. Accessed 1 July 2020. After consideration and seeking the advice of others, I have decided to leave the critique of Dr. Oliphint's former views intact. The reasons for doing so are at least two: first, because I critique proposals not persons, issues not individuals and second, because repudiating one's views does not undo the ill effects those views have had on others. In other words, it is my opinion that the proposals Dr. Oliphint has repudiated are alive and well in others who ought to be challenged.

from the WCF and SD, the text of the WCF and 2LCF are provided below. The reason why the text of the SD is not included is because it is nearly identical to the WCF at 4.1. It will be argued below that, though the WCF and 2LCF differ in form at 4.1, the doctrinal intent is substantially identical.

WCF 4.1	2LCF 4.1
It pleased God the Father, Son, and Holy Ghost, for the manifestation of the glory of his eternal power, wisdom, and goodness, in the beginning, to create, or make of nothing, the world, and all things therein, whether visible or invisible, in the space of six days, and all very good.	In the beginning it pleased God the Father, Son, and Holy Spirit, for the manifestation of the glory of His eternal power, wisdom, and goodness, to create or make the world, and all things therein, whether visible or invisible, in the space of six days, and all very good.

A FINAL WORD OF INTRODUCTION

This book is an attempt to bring its readers into the thought-world of the seventeenth-century confessional era concerning Trinity and creation, or God plus the world. The goal is not to stay in the seventeenth century, but to press upon readers the importance of the wisdom of the past for today. Too often in our day, we act as if the past has little, if anything, to offer us. It will be argued that this is not a safe place to stand. Instead, we ought to learn from the past and stand with it on the issue of God the creator. The Scriptures have been understood clearly by many who have gone before us on its most important issues. This book is written, in part, to assist its readers in realizing that the past has much for us from which to glean and with which we ought to agree. It will be contended that the manner whereby doctrinal statements were formulated in the seventeenth-century confessional era provides for us a helpful paradigm for both hermeneutics and theological method, both of which are worthy of retrieving and utilizing in our own day. The next chapter of the book, therefore, concentrates on hermeneutics and theological method.

2

Trinity and Creation

Hermeneutics and Method

THIS CHAPTER WILL CONSIDER the following: what is a confession of faith?; the intentional location of confession chapter 4; and the assumptions of chapter 4 and theological method. The confession is, obviously, a confession of faith. It is what those who subscribe it believe the Bible to teach. Each chapter is strategically placed. Each chapter assumes all that precedes it. These observations are, in one sense, simple and not difficult to prove. They are, however, very important, not only to make, but to explain and draw out some of their entailments.

WHAT IS A CONFESSION OF FAITH?

It is important to remind ourselves that the WCF, SD, and 2LCF are confessions of faith. They contain, in summary form, what subscribers to them believe the totality of the Bible teaches on given subjects. The confession is not merely a reference point from which one subsequently or further develops doctrinal conclusions; it is the doctrinal conclusions on the subjects which it addresses. Because the confession summarizes what the Bible teaches on given subjects, this means all of Holy Scripture is considered in the formulation of chapter 4. You can see this by noticing the Scripture references at 4.1. These texts are cited: John 1:2–3; Hebrews 1:2; Job 26:13; Romans 1:20;

Colossians 1:16; and Genesis 1:31. These are the Scripture references included in 2LCF. WCF includes these texts as well, and in this order: Genesis 1:2; Job 33:4; Jeremiah 10:12; Psalm 104:24; and Psalm 33:5–6.

These references display an unrestricted, canonical consultation while formulating 4.1. Citing Scripture references indicates to readers that the doctrinal formulation was made, in part, by the fruits of previous exegetical work in the biblical text. In other words, this is not some form of simplistic proof-texting. Indeed, it is far from it. Stefan T. Lindblad helps us understand the rationale behind the practice of citing biblical references in the confession. He says:

> A brief word is in order regarding the 2LCF's practice of citing biblical texts. To call this a "proof-texting method" in the modern derogatory sense is misleading. By citing specific texts in support of their statements, the authors of the Confession were indicating their adherence to methods of biblical interpretation and doctrinal formation that was characteristic not just of Reformed orthodoxy but also of the whole sweep of pre-critical exegesis. The texts cited here by the 2LCF are regarded as the primary seat of the doctrine, the primary (not exclusive) place in Scripture where the doctrine was either explicitly taught or "by just consequence deduced."[1] By citing these texts the 2LCF was not arbitrarily appealing to texts out of context. Rather, as with the other confessional symbols of the era, the 2LCF was drawing on the interpretation of these texts as argued in the biblical commentaries and annotations of the era. The statement of the Confession is thus a doctrinal result resting on the foundation of Scripture and its proper interpretation. The biblical texts cited thus point in two directions: back to biblical interpretation and forward to doctrinal formulation. Such texts, the *dicta probantia* or "proving statements," function as the necessary link between biblical interpretation and doctrinal formulation. A confession was not designed to reproduce the work of biblical interpretation, but to affirm its fruit, given that Scripture was the only authoritative and sufficient foundation for every doctrinal topic and for a system of theology as a whole. Thus, when the 2LCF cited [biblical texts], it was not employing a crude form of proof-texting, but was instead reflecting a whole tradition of

---

1. This is a citation from Nehemiah Coxe, *Vindiciae Veritatis, or a Confutation of the heresies and gross errours asserted by Thomas Collier in his additional word to his Body of Divinity* (London: for Nathaniel Ponder, 1677), 9.

interpretation understood to be utterly indispensable and foundational for this doctrinal construct.[2]

When the confession cites scriptural texts, it assumes exegetical labor and its fruit. It also assumes long-standing methods of biblical interpretation and doctrinal formulation. Lindblad's words, "The texts cited here by the 2LCF are regarded as the primary seat of the doctrine, the primary (not exclusive) place in Scripture where the doctrine was either explicitly taught or 'by just consequence deduced,'" are especially important for our study. This indicates to us that the texts cited are not the only scriptural bases from which the confessional formulations were derived. It also alerts us to the fact that the formulations are not mere recitations of the words of Scripture. Doctrines taught in Scripture must be formulated into words other than Scripture in order to explicate their meanings for us.

The use of Scripture in the formulation of the confession's statement on creation also indicates a distinct working hermeneutic (confessed in 1.9). This method of interpretation is an illustration of the analogy of faith. In other words, when formulating Christian doctrine, we must allow the totality of Scripture to speak prior to our formulations. We will return to this later. It is a very important issue.

THE INTENTIONAL LOCATION OF CHAPTER 4

It is important to note the place of chapter 4 in the confession. It comes immediately after the chapter titled "Of God's Decree." This is a deliberate placement. The decree of God is an *ad intra* divine work, as Richard A. Muller says, "willed by the entire Godhead as the foundation of all [*ad*

---

2. Stefan T. Lindblad, "'Eternally Begotten of the Father': An Analysis of the Second London Confession of Faith's Doctrine of the Eternal Generation of the Son," in *By Common Confession: Essays in Honor of James M. Renihan*, eds. Ronald S. Baines, Richard C. Barcellos, and James P. Butler (Palmdale, CA: RBAP, 2015), 338–39. In a footnote, Lindblad directs readers as follows: "For a helpful survey of the dependence of theological formulation on biblical interpretation, see Muller, *PRRD*, 2:442–520, esp. 502–20; and Richard A. Muller, 'Scripture and the Westminster Confession,' in Richard A. Muller and Rowland S. Ward, *Scripture and Worship: Biblical Interpretation and the Directory for Public Worship*, The Westminster Assembly and the Reformed Faith, vol. 1, ed. Carl R. Trueman (Phillipsburg, NJ: P&R Publishing, 2007), 59–82." *PRRD* is an abbreviation of *Post-Reformation Reformed Dogmatics*. In the Muller and Ward book, Muller says: ". . . the confession and the catechisms cite texts by way of referencing an exegetical tradition reaching back, in many cases, to the fathers of the church in the first five centuries of Christianity and, quite consistently, reflecting the path of biblical interpretation belonging to the Reformed tradition as it developed in the sixteenth century and in the beginning of the seventeenth" (81).

extra works]."[3] The decree is sometimes termed an immanent, or intrinsic, divine work because its termination is in God. The execution of God's decree, however, brings us into the realm of God's external, *ad extra*, transient, or extrinsic, works—works which produce effects, or creatures. What is meant by "creatures" from here on out is "anything other than God."[4] The external works of God are "those outgoing works whose term lies beyond the godhead."[5] These include creation (confession 4, "Of Creation") and providence (confession 5, "Of Divine Providence" through 32, "Of the Last Judgment"), or the works of nature and of grace. The *ad extra* works, in other words, include creation, conservation, re-creation, and consummation. Muller defines *ad extra* divine works as follows: "*the outward or external works of God*; the divine activities according to which God creates, sustains, . . . including the activity or work of grace and salvation."[6] The *ad extra* works of God are sometimes termed the divine economy (i.e., the execution of the divine plan for creation unto consummation). The divine economy is inclusive of creation, providence, the work of redemption or restoration (i.e., the renovation and perfection of spoiled nature), and the consummation. It is logically and pedagogically fitting to place chapter 4 after the decree and prior to divine providence.

THE ASSUMPTIONS OF CHAPTER 4 AND THEOLOGICAL METHOD

Since chapter 4 is not the first chapter of the confession, it assumes all the formulations which precede it. Though this is obvious to anyone who reads the confession, it is no small or trite observation. It has mammoth implications for hermeneutics and theological method in the process of formulating Christian doctrine.

Confession 4.1 Does Not Make Sense without the Previous Chapters

That 4.1 does not make sense without the previous chapters is obvious, for example, when it says, "In the beginning it pleased God the Father, Son, and

---

3. Richard A. Muller, *Dictionary of Latin and Greek Theological Terms*, Second Edition (Grand Rapids: Baker Academic, 1985, 2017), 245.

4. Ian A. McFarland, *From Nothing: A Theology of Creation* (Louisville: Westminster John Knox Press, 2014), 59.

5. Webster, *God without Measure*, 1:89.

6. Muller, *Dictionary*, 244.

Holy Spirit." This assumes all of chapter 2, "Of God and of the Holy Trinity," particularly paragraph three on the blessed Trinity, which reads as follows:

> In this divine and infinite Being there are three subsistences, the Father, the Word (or Son), and Holy Spirit, of one substance, power, and eternity, each having the whole Divine essence, yet the essence undivided, the Father is of none, neither begotten nor proceeding, the Son is eternally begotten of the Father, the Holy Spirit proceeding from the Father and the Son, all infinite, without beginning, therefore but one God, who is not to be divided in nature and Being; but distinguished by several peculiar, relative properties, and personal relations; which doctrine of the Trinity is the foundation of all our communion with God, and comfortable dependence on him.

Chapter 4.1 continues: ". . . for the manifestation of the glory of His eternal power, wisdom, and goodness." Divine eternity (WCF/2LCF 2.1), divine power (WCF/2LCF 2.1), divine wisdom (WCF/2LCF 2.1), and divine goodness (WCF/2LCF 2.2) are confessed in chapter 2. What chapter 4 does is confess, in particular, the *manifestation* of the *very same God* confessed in chapter 2. This manifestation of God comprises the revelatory divine effects in creatures. It is the eternal and immutable God confessed in chapter 2 who manifests divine power, wisdom, and goodness in that which comes-to-be. Not only that, but it is God—Father, Son, and Holy Spirit—who creates to manifest himself in, by, and upon creatures (see WCF/2LCF 2.2, "only manifesting His own glory in, by, unto, and upon [creatures]"). In other words, the God confessed in chapter 2 does not newly fashion himself in order to create and manifest himself, thereby becoming the God confessed in chapter 4 (or any other chapter in the confession). God is; he does not come-to-be in any sense. There is no need for the God of chapter 2 to add anything to himself in order to create and manifest himself as the God of chapter 4. In fact, it is impossible for God to newly fashion himself in any sense whatsoever. As Steven J. Duby says, ". . . there is no chance of God's outward actions producing two versions of the Trinity . . ."[7] Since "in God there is only God,"[8] since it is the eternal God who creates, since the eternal

---

7. Steven J. Duby, *God in Himself: Scripture, Metaphysics, and the Task of Christian Theology* (Downers Grove, IL: IVP Academic, 2019), 185.

8. Matthew Levering, *Engaging the Doctrine of Creation: Cosmos, Creatures, and the Wise and Good Creator* (Grand Rapids: Baker Academic, 2017), 24. Levering is citing Henri de Lubac, *The Mystery of the Supernatural*. Similar to de Lubac, in the eighteenth century, John Gill asserted this: ". . . as it is commonly said, whatever is in God, is God . . ." John Gill, *A Body of Doctrinal and Practical Divinity* (Paris AR: The Baptist Standard Bearer, 1989), 256–57.

God who creates is immutable, and since the eternal and immutable God who creates is triune, or just is the Trinity, then all that is God is that which creates in order to execute the divine decree. It is just God who creates. Creation, then, is an effect of the eternally and immutably powerful God, an effect of eternal divine wisdom, and an effect of eternal divine goodness. Indeed, creation is an effect of the Trinity. As John Webster puts it: "[Creation] is a common work of the undivided Trinity; there are not three creators. But there are [quoting Emery] 'three who create.'"[9]

When 4.1 is confessed, therefore, one asserts that creation manifests or, in the language of Psalm 19, it *tells* or *declares* to us something, at least (see Rom. 1:20), of the eternal power, wisdom, and goodness of God, though without words. We call this general revelation (see WCF/2LCF 1.1). And though the work of creation (indeed, the entire divine economy) also tells us something about the persons of the Trinity in their relation one to another (to be discussed subsequently), we do not know *that* or *what* it tells us about those relations apart from special revelation, that is, Holy Scripture. The Trinity, we must affirm, is an article of faith, not accessible through nature alone. Divine effects, creatures, or general revelation, reveal something of God to us, they tell us something about the God who effects or who causes them to be (Rom. 1:20). Creatures even tell us something about the persons of the Godhead. This will be teased-out in subsequent discussion. For now, it is important to affirm also that the Bible itself, written by various human authors in Hebrew, Aramaic, and Greek, and in the form in which it has been handed-down to us, is not God (i.e., it is not eternal, not immortal, not invisible, not comprehensive of the divine wisdom, etc). The Bible is the written Word of God, written by men, and in that sense is, therefore, a creature of God (i.e., written words are creature not Creator). This means that, as creature, the Bible tells us something about God and that which is not God, as well as telling us something about the persons of the glorious Trinity and the triune work of what we call creation.

Because this may be new to some, it may need to be explored a bit more. It is important for our discussion at this point and later. Our theology is that of creatures. It was given to us by our Creator. It came into being. Franciscus Junius defines this type of theology as ectypal. He says, "Ectypal theology . . . is the wisdom of divine matters, *fashioned* by God from the archetype of Himself, through the communication of grace for His own glory."[10] Our theology is not eternal as to its form; it was "fashioned by

9. Webster, *God without Measure*, 1:98. We will discuss creation as a work of the undivided Trinity below.

10. Franciscus Junius, *A Treatise on True Theology*, trans. David C. Noe (Grand Rapids: Reformation Heritage Books, 2014), 113; emphasis added. See Muller, *Dictionary*, 360–61.

God," though it does reflect the Eternal's knowledge. It came into existence, though being "created according to the capacity of the one communicating it"[11] and "communicated to things created, according to the capacity of the created things themselves."[12] We know divine effects according to our creaturely capacities. This is not the case with God. And the divine effects we know in the form of Holy Scripture are delivered to us "at various times and in various ways spoke[n] in time past to the fathers by the prophets, [and] has [been] in these last days spoken to us by *His* Son" (Heb. 1:1–2a). This coming-to-us form of spoken and written revelation is creature. It was created by God for us, in accordance with our receptive and interpretive capacities.

Though the Bible is the inspired, written Word of God, it was written *by* men and *for* men. Though it is God's theology for us, it is not God's theology of God as God knows God and all things in relation to God. That kind of theology is termed archetypal. Archetypal theology "is the divine wisdom of divine matters."[13] Whereas we are eyewitnesses of created things and obtain knowledge of God by them, this is not the case with God's wisdom or knowledge. Divine wisdom and knowledge are not obtained. As Junius says, "[The divine] wisdom produces intellect, reason, conclusions, knowledge, and wisdom itself in others" but "[i]t is not born from them."[14] Archetypal theology is the comprehensive divine knowledge of God and all things in relation to him. This means that the Bible does not, and cannot, give us comprehensive knowledge of God. Only God comprehends God (1 Cor. 2:10–11). The finite cannot contain the infinite. We may and do apprehend some knowledge of God but our finitude (and sinfulness) precludes us from knowing God as God knows God in himself. It also means that the knowledge the Bible gives us is accommodated to our creaturely capacities. Accommodated knowledge is what we call revelation. This means that, as stated above, the Bible is a creature of God and as creature tells us something about God and that which is not God, as well as telling us something about the persons of the glorious Trinity and the triune work which we call creation.

Chapter 4, "Of Creation," is a confession of the execution of that which is confessed explicitly in chapter 3, "Of God's Decree." It also assumes chapters 1 (i.e., the Word of God written) and 2 (i.e., the God of the written Word). One of the entailments of this is that, before one can adequately

---

11. Junius, *A Treatise on True Theology*, 116.
12. Junius, *A Treatise on True Theology*, 117.
13. Junius, *A Treatise on True Theology*, 107. See Muller, *Dictionary*, 359–60.
14. Junius, *A Treatise on True Theology*, 108.

account for what Scripture teaches about divine creation, a robust, fully-formed theology proper (especially of the doctrine of the Trinity) must be firmly in place. Consider Webster again:

> God's outer works are most fully understood as loving and purposive when set against the background of his utter sufficiency—against the fact that *no external operation or relation can constitute or augment his life*, which is already infinitely replete. Once this is grasped, the nature of creaturely being begins to disclose itself as pure benefit, intelligible only as God is known and loved in his inherent completeness.[15]

The italicized words above are crucial for our discussion. Webster says, "no external operation or relation can constitute or augment his life." God manifests himself by his *ad extra* works but in no sense constitutes or augments himself in order to do so or while doing so. This important point will be developed later.

Though we learn of God in the economy, God's external or outer works, we cannot account properly for those works without a theology of the One who works prior to accounting for them. Webster rightly claims the core of the doctrine of creation is theology proper.[16] E. L. Mascall claims something similar.

> Logically and essentially, the doctrine of God is the fundamental doctrine of the Christian Religion, for, according to its teaching, everything other than God depends upon him and exists for his glory.[17]

Without allowing first place to theology proper, we cannot make sense of the cosmological assertions of Scripture, nor, in particular, its anthropomorphic language pertaining to divine action (e.g., "the Spirit of God was *hovering*" [Gen. 1:2; emphasis added]; "Then God *said*" [Gen. 1:3; emphasis

---

15. Webster, *God without Measure*, 1:6; emphasis added. A better, more technically precise, word than "inherent" is "intrinsic," since nothing actually or really inheres in God. Thanks to James E. Dolezal for this observation. See Bernard Wuellner, *Dictionary of Scholastic Philosophy* (Fitzwilliam, NH: Loreto Publications, 2012), 61, where the entrance for "inherence" reads as follows: "existence in another being as in a subject of being or as a modification of another being. Accidents are said to inhere in substance" and 64, where the entrance for "intrinsic" reads as follows: "1. pertaining to the nature of a thing or person; constitutive. 2. contained or being within; internal. 3. inherent." The third meaning listed for "intrinsic" should cause a brief pause in us to chide Webster too much.

16. See Webster, *God without Measure*, 1:84.

17. E. L. Mascall, *He Who Is: A Study in Traditional Theism* (London, New York, Toronto: Longmans, Green and Co., 1943), 1.

added]; "the *sound* of the LORD God *walking* in the garden" [Gen. 3:8; emphasis added]; and the heavens as "the work of [God's] *fingers*" [Psalm 8:3; emphasis added]). We must have a robust theology proper in place in order to account properly for divine fingers. Even Genesis 1:1, "In the beginning God created the heavens and the earth," requires first place to theology proper. Without it, one might conclude God became tired due to the magnitude of the work of creation. Webster continues, "What Christian theology says about creation is a function of what it says about God, and what it says about God is a function of what it hears from God."[18] We must hear from God about who he is before we can account for what he does. If one gets theology proper wrong, errors in other places of systematic theology are inevitable. Mascall makes this point clear.

> since . . . the doctrine of God is the basis upon which all other
> Christian doctrine rests, any error that has been allowed to creep
> into a man's belief about God will distort his understanding of
> every other Christian truth. If his idea of God is wrong, his idea
> of Christ will be wrong, since Christ is God incarnate . . .[19]

Let us explore the place of theology proper a bit more, for it further confirms the importance of hermeneutics and theological method when confessing trinitarian creation.

The Method of the Confession Is the Method the Bible Itself Demands

We are confronted with the necessity of the priority of theology proper (i.e., that and what God *is*) to account for the economy (i.e., that and what God *does*) in the first verse of the Bible: "In the beginning *God* created the heavens and the earth" (Gen. 1:1; emphasis added). What is intended by the word "God"? Does the plural form of God in the Hebrew text (i.e., Elohim) and the singular verb (i.e., "created") hint at a plurality of persons in the Godhead or not? What does it mean that he "created"? The same goes for the second verse of the Bible: "And the *Spirit of God* was *hovering* over the face of the waters" (Gen. 1:2; emphasis added). Who or what is this "Spirit of God" and what is meant by "hovering"? And the same goes for verse 3,

---

18. Webster, *God without Measure*, 1:84. It could also be put this way: "What Christian theology says about creation, conservation, re-creation, and consummation is a function of what it says about God, and what it says about God is a function of what it hears from God." Remember, the doctrine of the Trinity is a distributed doctrine. It conditions all subsequent *loci*.

19. Mascall, *He Who Is*, 2–3.

"Then God *said* . . ." (Gen. 1:3; emphasis added). God speaks? Does he speak Hebrew or some sort of divine language?

What is being asserted is this: divine ontology precedes divine economy and conditions our interpretation of it.[20] When divine ontology does not inform properly the divine economy in our interpretive efforts, a theological train-wreck is in the making that will end up in the junk-yard of heresy. For how would one explain "Then God *said*" (emphasis added) without more information about the One who said, "Let there be light" (Gen. 1:3)? Without more information, one might conclude that God (whoever he or whatever it is) must have vocal chords, a larynx, or voice box, and that he takes in air and it flows over throat organs which end up producing audible sounds that come forth from a mouth producing detectible and understandable words. Though explaining how to account for this text is "putting the cart before the horse" in the context of our discussion, a comment by Matthew Poole may introduce readers to the manner by which seventeenth-century expositors of Scripture dealt with anthropomorphic language pertaining to divine works related to creation. Poole's interpretation of this text is a good example of the method advocated in later discussion. He says:

> He commanded, not by such a word or speech as we use, which agreeth not with the spiritual nature of God; but either by an act of his powerful will, called *the word of his power*, Heb. i. 3; or, by his substantial Word, his *Son, by whom he made the worlds*, Heb. i. 2; Psal. xxxiii. 6, who is called, *The Word*, partly, if not principally, for this reason, John i. 1—3, 10.[21]

Consider verse 26 as well: "Let *Us* make man in *Our* image, according to *Our* likeness" (Gen. 1:26; emphasis added). One might conclude from these words a plurality of creators without more information, or some sort

---

20. In private, written discussion on this issue, a friend gave me this important feedback: "In giving a proper and systematic account of the order of being, we must begin with God. But in the order of knowing we begin with creation, i.e., Scripture and the things that are made." I think my discussion reflects this very point. Mascall provides these helpful words: "'The Catholic Faith is this,' declares the Athanasian Creed, 'that we worship one God in Trinity and Trinity in Unity.' This does not mean, however, that the truth of the triune being of God is the first thing of which most of us become conscious in our life as Christians. One of the drawbacks of being a mere creature is that you see everything the wrong way round; you look at things from man's standpoint and not from God's. The order in which things ultimately exist, the *ordo essendi*, is usually the precise opposite of the order in which we come to know them, the *ordo cognoscendi*; and that is specially true of that which is of all beings the most fundamental, namely God himself" (Mascall, *He Who Is*, 1).

21. Matthew Poole, *A Commentary on the Whole Bible, Volume I: Genesis–Job* (Edinburgh; Carlisle, PA: The Banner of Truth Trust, Reprinted 1974), 2.

of pre-cosmological, heavenly sanhedrin inclusive of God and others.[22] What is the point? We cannot interpret properly the divine economy, God's external works, the *opera Dei ad extra*, unless we have theology proper (God, Trinity, and decree) firmly in place. Without this, we run the risk of becoming some sort of neo-Socinians. Webster is correct when he says, "We do not understand the economy unless we take time to consider God who is, though creatures might not have been."[23]

Maybe asking and answering an important question at this juncture will help illustrate what is being argued. Where do we learn of God as Trinity, for example? In the economy. This means, as Giles Emery asserts, "[t]he doctrine of the Trinity and the history of salvation are intimately connected; they mutually illuminate each other."[24] It is through the economy that the Trinity is revealed to us and it is the Trinity throughout the economy which illuminates it for us.[25] The acts of God (i.e., *oikonomia*) reveal the divine to us, but the *theologia* (i.e., the mystery of God as Trinity), as revealed in Scripture, illuminates all the acts of God.[26] The Trinity constitutes the economy, not the other way around. Though the economy reveals the Trinity, it does not make or re-make the Trinity. Emery's comments may be helpful:

22. The idea of a "heavenly sanhedrin" comes from John Owen, *The Works of John Owen*, 23 vols., ed. William H. Goold (Edinburgh; Carlisle, PA: The Banner of Truth Trust, 1991 edition), 17:222. He argues that God is clearly the exclusive creator (ref. to Gen. 1:26), not a heavenly court inclusive of angels, "as if God had a sanhedrim in heaven . . ." The spelling of *sanhedrim* is original in Owen. The Belgic Confession of 1561 comments on Gen. 1:26 as follows: "From this saying, Let *us* make man in *our* image, it appears that there are more persons than one in the Godhead; and when He says, 'God created,' He signifies the unity. It is true; He does not say how many persons there are, but that which appears to us somewhat obscure in the Old Testament is very plain in the New." James T. Dennison, Jr., *Reformed Confessions of the 16th and 17th Centuries in English Translation*, Volume 2, 1552–1566 (Grand Rapids: Reformation Heritage Books, 2010), 429. This shows that Owen's view was not novel and is included in the Reformed confessional tradition.

23. Webster, *God without Measure*, 1:86.

24. Gilles Emery, *The Trinity: An Introduction to Catholic Doctrine on the Triune God* (Washington, D.C.: The Catholic University of America Press, 2011), 173.

25. This is my attempt to paraphrase the *Catechism of the Catholic Church* where it says, "Through the *oikonomia* the *theologia* is revealed to us; but conversely, the *theologia* illuminates the whole *oikonomia*," as quoted in Emery, *Trinity*, 160.

26. For a helpful discussion on the history and meaning of the terms *theologia* and *oikonomia* see Lewis Ayres, "[Common Places] Pro-Nicene Theology: Theologia and Oikonomia," https://zondervanacademic.com/blog/common-places-theologia-and-oikonomia-by-lewis-ayres/. Accessed 6 September 2017. For a good discussion on the more recent and common terminology (i.e., economic Trinity and immanent Trinity) see Fred Sanders, *The Triune God*, New Studies in Dogmatics, Michael Allen and Scott R. Swain, gen. eds. (Grand Rapids: Zondervan, 2016), 144–53. Sanders provides resistance to the newer terminology.

> God reveals himself . . . as Trinity, because he is in himself Trin-
> ity and he acts as he is; however, the reception of the revelation
> of God . . . in the economy does not exhaust the mystery of the
> Trinity in itself.[27]

In order to account properly for God's acts *in* the economy, we must learn who God is *from* the economy. Our interpretation of the economy must be conditioned by who God is apart from it, though revealed to us in it.[28] And, as Emery says, God "is in himself Trinity and he acts as he is." Knowledge of who God *is*, then, must condition and shape our explanation of what God *does*. While this is so, we must always remember that "the economy does not exhaust the mystery of the Trinity in itself," as Emery asserts. Though God reveals himself through various revelatory modalities (to be discussed in a later chapter), the various revelatory divine acts do not exhaust who and what God is. As Webster says:

> The divine agent of revelatory acts is not fully understood if the
> phenomenality of those acts is treated as something primordial,
> a wholly sufficient presentation of the agent. God's outer works
> bear a surplus within themselves; they refer back to the divine
> agent who exceeds them.[29]

Though it is God who reveals himself in the economy, the revelation is not comprehensive of who and what he is, though it is true. As well, the acts of God are not "a wholly sufficient presentation of the agent," as Webster asserts. Or, as Duby says, "To put it rather crudely, there is more to God than what takes place in the economy."[30] The acts reveal God but do not exhaust his identity, nor do they constitute him as God. God is not God in virtue of what he does. Without the interpretive priority of *theologia* to *oikonomia*, we run the risk of reading the economy back into the divine ontology or ending up with two Trinities. This is the error of all forms of process theism and that of the older Socinians.

27. Emery, *Trinity*, 177.

28. See Duby, *God in Himself* for a book-length argument which supports my claim: "Our interpretation of the economy must be conditioned by who God is apart from it, though revealed to us in it." For example, Duby states the purpose of his book as follows: "The purpose of the book is to offer, on the basis of the Bible's account of human knowledge of God in the arc of redemptive history, a sketch of the rationale and practice of Christian reflection on God himself in his transcendence of the economy, which will enable us to reframe the roles of natural theology, metaphysics, and the incarnation in the doctrine of God" (6).

29. Webster, *God without Measure*, 1:8.

30. Duby, *God in Himself*, 16. The chapter title from which this is taken is "*Theologia* Within the Divine Economy" and is highly recommended.

Unfortunately, the method advocated above of privileging the ontological assertions of Scripture over the economic has received some resistance in our day. The justification for the older method is cogently argued in
the first two chapters of the book *Confessing the Impassible God: The Biblical,
Classical, & Confessional Doctrine of Divine Impassibility*. Those chapters
were written by Charles J. Rennie and Ronald S. Baines. The chapters are
highly recommended for your consideration. For example, Baines says, "To
suggest that giving precedence to the texts which speak of God ontologically
. . . is methodologically flawed, as Carson does, simply does not follow."[31]
Baines' statement is in response to these words by D. A. Carson.

> The methodological problem with the argument for divine
> impassibility is that it selects certain texts of Scripture, namely
> those that insist on God's sovereignty and changelessness, con-
> structs a theological grid on the basis of those selected texts, and
> then uses this grid to filter out all other texts, in particular those
> that speak of God's emotions. These latter texts, nicely filtered
> out, are then labeled "anthropomorphisms" and are written off.[32]

Baines responds as follows:

> What is perplexing with Carson's objections to both classical
> impassibility and present day versions of passibility is that he
> fails to provide a hermeneutical framework for dealing with the
> biblical material.[33]

---

31. Ronald S. Baines, "Hermeneutics: *Analogia Scripturae* and *Analogia Fidei*," in
*Confessing the Impassible God: The Biblical, Classical, & Confessional Doctrine of Di-
vine Impassibility*, eds. Ronald S. Baines, Richard C. Barcellos, James P. Butler, Stefan T.
Lindblad, and James M. Renihan (Palmdale, CA: RBAP, 2015), 86.

32. D. A. Carson, *How Long, O Lord?: Reflections on Suffering and Evil* (Grand Rapids: Baker Publishing Group, 2006), 165. Elsewhere, responding to classical Christian
impassibilists, Carson says: "You may then rest in God's sovereignty, but you can no
longer rejoice in his love. You may rejoice only in a linguistic expression that is an
accommodation of some reality of which we cannot conceive, couched in the anthropopathism of love. Give me a break. Paul did not pray that his readers might be able to
grasp the height and depth and length and breadth of an anthropopathism and know
this anthropopathism that surpasses knowledge (Eph. 3:14–21)." See D. A. Carson, *The
Difficult Doctrine of the Love of God* (Wheaton, IL: Crossway Books, 2000), 59. Baines
responds to this with these appropriate words: "While we will deal with this in greater
detail below, no classical impassibilist that we have encountered reads Paul this way.
Doesn't Paul affirm that the love he wants the Ephesians to know is that which 'surpasses knowledge'?" (Baines, "Hermeneutics: *Analogia Scripturae* and *Analogia Fidei*," 84).

33. Baines, "Hermeneutics: *Analogia Scripturae* and *Analogia Fidei*," 83.

The issue is method, as Baines implies; and method is the very reason why the denial of privileging the ontological assertions of Scripture over the economic is brought up at this point.

How do we account for the biblical material that at face value seems contradictory? For when considering divine creation, we must account for "When I consider Your heavens, the work of Your fingers" (Psalm 8:3), and for the fact that God is "the King eternal, immortal, invisible" (1 Tim. 1:17). Divine fingers and divine invisibility, at face value, seem contradictory. A hermeneutical framework for dealing with the biblical material must be in place or one is bound to confess that God has literal wings, for example, because in Psalm 17:8 we read, "Hide me under the shadow of Your wings." Either God actually does have literal, really existing wings or this must be some sort of ornithomorphism (i.e., the analogical attribution of birdly traits to God). Surely no one wants to assert that God has literal or real eternal wings and "[s]urely [no one wants to] believe that God temporarily or permanently assumed the intermediary properties of feathered appendages," as Cameron G. Porter asserts.[34] Though the principle of privileging the ontological scriptural assertions of God over the metaphorical has received resistance from some in our day, the confession itself is an illustration of this very method. Let me prove this assertion.

The confession lays the groundwork for understanding the divine economy by first establishing its interpretive basis in theology proper, and the doctrine of the written Word of God. Prior to discussing the external operations of God, the confession contains foundational statements concerning the ontology and *ad intra* works of God, the very same God who operates *ad extra*. These statements are made *prior to* statements about God's external operations.[35] For example, consider the following statements from chapter 2, "Of God and of the Holy Trinity":

> The Lord our God *is* but one living and true God . . . (2LCF 2.1; emphasis added)

---

34. Cameron G. Porter, "*The Majesty of Mystery: Celebrating the Glory of an Incomprehensible God,* A Review Article," *Journal of the Institute of Reformed Baptist Studies* (2017): 92–93. Porter's article is included as an appendix to this book.

35. In private, written discussion on this issue, a friend gave me this important feedback: "The order of the confession (in treating God before creatures) is logically arranged to reflect the order of *principia,* not to explain the epistemic route of humans in coming to the knowledge of God." His point is that the confession is logically and pedagogically arranged according to the *principia theologiae,* the fundamental principles of theology (i.e., Scripture and God). See Muller, *Dictionary,* 288–89. The epistemic route taken in coming to the knowledge of God, however, begins with creatures (e.g., our minds, creation, Scripture).

> God, *having* all life, glory, goodness, blessedness, in and of Himself, *is* alone in and unto Himself all-sufficient . . . (2LCF 2.2; emphasis added)

> In this divine and infinite Being there *are* three subsistences, the Father, the Word (or Son), and Holy Spirit, of one substance, power, and eternity, each *having* the whole divine essence, yet the essence undivided . . . (2LCF 2.3; emphasis added).

These metaphysical, ontological assertions concerning who God *is* condition our explanations of what God *does*. The confession displays a theological method which itself gives priority to who God is (i.e., ontology) before it tells us what God does (i.e., economy). This means that anyone who subscribes the WCF, SD, or 2LCF and denies the interpretive priority of the ontological to the economic implicitly contradicts the method of their confession, though maybe unwittingly. By the way, this method of giving priority to God *in himself* over God *for us* is amply reflected in any systematic theology textbook worth owning and consulting.

Texts like Genesis 1:1, 2, 3, and 26 not only require the priority of theology proper over the interpretation of God's economy, they require a doctrine of the written Word, inclusive of a theory of its interpretation. Consider these words from chapter 1 of the confession:

> The Holy Scripture is the only sufficient, certain, and infallible rule of all saving knowledge, faith, and obedience. (2LCF 1.1a)

> The infallible rule of interpretation of Scripture is the Scripture itself; and therefore when there is a question about the true and full sense of any Scripture (which is not manifold but one), it must be searched by other places that speak more clearly. (2LCF 1.9)

Assuming the truthfulness of these assertions, nothing other than Holy Scripture presents man with "the only sufficient, certain, and infallible rule of all saving knowledge, faith, and obedience" and nothing other than Holy Scripture interprets itself infallibly. So, when seeking to explain creation and accounting for God's *ad extra* works, we must not shelve our doctrine of the written Word and its interpretation, just as we must not shelve theology proper while doing the same.

It is important to affirm that Scripture is the written Word of God. As such, it often records divine acts after the execution of divine acts *and* explains them to us via the form of written words. In other words, God acts then God both *records* his acts and *interprets* his acts in Holy Scripture. Scripture, being fully inspired by God, is our only infallible, written revelation *and interpretation* of who God is and what he does. Since God is the author of Scripture, it is God who tells us in Scripture who he is and what he has done. As soon as we see the word "God" in Scripture we ought to ask, "Who is this God who created the heavens and the earth?" Once we ask that question, the track we must follow for an answer will lead us (back) into the study of theology proper. While studying the confession, the answer to the question, "Who is this God who created the heavens and the earth?," refers us back to chapters 2 and 3, "Of God and of the Holy Trinity" and "Of God's Decree." The confession employs a distinct theological method at this juncture. Webster's words are to the point:

> . . . the doctrine of creation concerns an external work of God, it refers back to prior teaching about . . . God's inner life. Reflection on creation therefore requires clarity about some primary topics in trinitarian theology: the relation of essence and persons, the distinction between immanent and transitive divine acts, the indivisibility of the *opera ad extra*.[36]

Interestingly, though the confession leads us from chapter 4 back to chapters 1 through 3 in order to account for the God who creates, the Bible forces us to go from Genesis 1:1, the God who creates, to subsequent Scripture, in order to account for the identity and creative acts of the God of Genesis 1:1.

We Must Interpret Scripture Texts in Dialogue with Scripture Texts

We cannot interpret properly what God does, recorded for us in Scripture, unless we know something of the God who effects what is recorded for us in Scripture. In other words, there must be a hermeneutical, interpretive dialogue between the text which confronts us (e.g., Gen. 1:1, 2, 3, and 26) and other texts which inform us about who the God of those texts is and how he works. There must be a hermeneutical dialogue, or circle, that we not only recognize and respect but must consistently employ, if we want to speak of God as God has revealed himself in his written Word. Done properly, this will keep interpreters from making statements which contradict Scripture, such as the crude example above, that God must have vocal chords, a larynx, or voice box, and a mouth. Since Moses tells us that God spoke, yet we are told elsewhere in Scripture that God is invisible (e.g., 1 Tim. 1:17 and 6:16) and spirit and therefore immaterial (e.g., John 4:24), we

36. Webster, *God without Measure*, 1:83.

must account for both, and accounting for both often requires hearing from God from other texts different from the ones under consideration. Giving priority to ontological affirmations about God will keep us from becoming neo-anthropomorphites, guarding us from the naive biblicism that is present and becoming more prevalent in our day.[37]

To whet your appetite a bit and introduce you to an issue that will be discussed later, notice Genesis 1:2 again: "And the *Spirit of God* was *hovering* over the face of the waters" (emphasis added). Assuming the translation is accurate (and I think it is), how should we go about explaining this? What or who is the Spirit of God and how can we best account for the fact that Moses asserts "the Spirit of God was *hovering* over the face of the waters" (emphasis added)? Is this some sort of primordial, quasi-divine, pneumatological hover-craft given creative power? Or is this an operation of the Holy Spirit independent of the Father and the Son? How should we account for these things? What is the most important written source outside Genesis 1:2 we ought to consult for help? The answer should be obvious. We should consult Scripture, for Scripture not only records divine acts for us, *it interprets divine acts for us and explains who and what the divine agent who acts is*. As well, since Scripture is the written Word of God, infallible and inerrant, when it interprets previously recorded divine acts it does so infallibly. In other words, there are places in Holy Scripture where we have the Word of God on the Word of God. We have "divinely inspired and infallible interpretation by the divine author himself," to quote a friend. John Owen says, "The only unique, public, authentic, and infallible interpreter of Scripture is none other than the Author of Scripture Himself . . . that is, God the Holy Spirit."[38] The Bible's interpretation of itself is infallible. When it utilizes itself in any fashion, it is God's interpretation for us and, therefore, the divine revelation of how texts should be understood by men. This often means that later texts shed interpretive light on earlier texts, and upon the divine agent and acts contained in those texts. This occurs not only when the New Testament consults the Old Testament, but it occurs in the Old Testament itself. This will be illustrated in later discussion. We could put it this way: subsequent revelation often makes explicit what is implicit in antecedent

---

37. For informed discussions on biblicism see James M. Renihan, "Person and Place: Two Problems with Biblicism," in *Southern California Reformed Baptist Pastors' Conference Papers*, Volume I (2012), ed. Richard C. Barcellos (Palmdale, CA: RBAP, 2012), 111–27 and Michael Allen and Scott R. Swain, *Reformed Catholicity: The Promise of Retrieval for Theology and Biblical Interpretation* (Grand Rapids: Baker Academic, 2015), 84ff. and 117–41.

38. John Owen, *Biblical Theology or The Nature, Origin, Development, and Study of Theological Truth in Six Books* (Pittsburgh, PA: Soli Deo Gloria Publications, 1994), 797.

revelation. In the words of Vern S. Poythress, "The later communications build on the earlier. What is implicit in the earlier often becomes explicit in the later."[39]

Let us consider Genesis 1:2 once again. While Genesis 1:2 says, "And the Spirit of God was hovering over the face of the waters," Psalm 104:24 says, "O LORD, how manifold are Your works! In wisdom You have made them all. The earth is full of Your possessions—" and in verse 30 we read, "You send forth Your Spirit, they are created; And You renew the face of the earth." In Job 26:13 we read, "By His Spirit He adorned the heavens." These texts (and there are others) outside of Genesis echo it and further explain it to and for us. These are instances of inner-biblical exegesis within the Old Testament.

When the Bible exegetes the Bible, therefore, we have an infallible interpretation because of the divine author of Scripture. Scripture not only records the acts of God, it also interprets them. If we are going to explain the acts of God in creation, God's initial economy, with any hope of accurately accounting for those acts, we must first know something of the triune God who acts. And the only written source of infallible knowledge of the triune God who acts is the Bible and the Bible alone.

CONCLUDING THOUGHTS: THREE WAYS TO RETRIEVE A THEOLOGICAL METHOD THAT WILL SERVE THE CHURCH WELL

It should be clear by now that hermeneutics and theological method are of utmost importance in our dogmatic reflections and assertions on the Trinity and creation. Three ways we can retrieve a theological method that will be of service to the church will now be offered.

We Must Respect the Theological Grammar of the Christian Theological Tradition

First, if we are going to retrieve a theological method that serves the church well, we must respect the theological grammar of the Christian theological tradition. This is exactly what the confession does. It is displayed, for example, in the triad of 4.1, "power, wisdom, and goodness," which will be

---

39. See Vern S. Poythress, "Biblical Hermeneutics," in *Seeing Christ in all of Scripture: Hermeneutics at Westminster Theological Seminary*, ed. Peter A. Lillback (Philadelphia, PA: Westminster Seminary Press, 2016), 14.

explained in later discussion. This triad has a distinct history in the context of discussing the Trinity and creation. The method of the confession includes the utilization of technical terms and phrases, *and the meaning of those terms and phrases*, as received from previous generations. In other words, when it uses old words, the confession implies the old and received meanings of those words. It uses old words in order to show continuity with the past and with others in the seventeenth century. It does this in order not to clog religion with new words or novel doctrines.

All of that is to say we must not impose new meanings on old words, or more basic etymological meanings on technical, theological words. Doing so wreaks havoc on the system of doctrine in which those terms are used. If we want to retrieve both the doctrine and method of the confession (and I think we should), we need to respect the theological grammar of the Christian theological tradition. If we are going to use and define terms or phrases (and we should and must), we must not argue their meanings from mere etymology or *Webster's Dictionary*. Instead, our first place to go for the definition of technical, theological terms and phrases while studying the confession ought to be Richard A. Muller's *Dictionary of Latin and Greek Theological Terms* in its latest edition. Another helpful resource for interpreting the confession is James M. Renihan's *A Toolkit for Confessions: Helps for the Study of English Puritan Confessions of Faith*.[40]

We Must Understand the Difference between Biblical Theology and Systematic Theology

Second, if we are going to retrieve a theological method that serves the church well, we must understand the difference between biblical theology and systematic theology. Once we recognize the difference, we will have to admit that, when formulating Christian doctrine, biblical theology has built-in limitations. These limitations are self-induced by it which inhibit it from the task of creating fully-formed doctrinal statements.

To further explain what is meant by the previous paragraph, it will do us well to consider Geerhardus Vos's view of biblical theology. Vos begins his definition of biblical theology with these words: "Biblical Theology is that branch of Exegetical Theology which deals with the *process* of the self-revelation of God deposited in the Bible."[41] Note the word "process."

---

40. James M. Renihan, *A Toolkit for Confessions: Helps for the Study of English Puritan Confessions of Faith* (Palmdale, CA: RBAP, 2017).

41. Geerhardus Vos, *Biblical Theology: Old and New Testaments* (1948; reprint, Grand Rapids: Wm. B. Eerdmans Publishing Company, June 1988), 5; emphasis added.

This entails that biblical theology, unlike systematic theology, finds as its working materials the history of redemption in process as delivered to us in the Holy Scriptures. This includes accounting for historic progress, organic development, covenantal expansiveness, Christ-centeredness, and a multiplicity of genres.[42] In other words, biblical theology is not the same as, and does not produce the fruits of, systematic theology. It hands its labors to the systematician in order to be used by him, but its fruit looks different because its purpose and method is different. It is interesting to note, by the way, that Vos wrote *both* a dogmatics *and* a biblical theology. These works display differing methods of treating the Bible and offer differing, though not competing, analyses of its teaching. This should not surprise us. Systematic theology deals with the Bible subject-by-subject, or topic-by-topic, as a finished product; this biblical theology does not and cannot do if it is to be true to itself.

Let me allow Vos to speak for himself. Describing the relationship between biblical and systematic theology, he says:

> There is no difference in that one would be more closely bound to the Scriptures than the other. In this they are wholly alike. Nor does the difference lie in this, that the one transforms the Biblical material, whereas the other would leave it unmodified. Both equally make the truth deposited in the Bible undergo a transformation: but the difference arises from the fact that the principles by which the transformation is effected differ. In Biblical Theology the principle is one of historical, in Systematic Theology it is one of logical construction. Biblical Theology draws a *line* of development. Systematic Theology draws a *circle*.[43]

So, for example, bringing this discussion into our own day, when James E. Dolezal writes, "But it seems to me that biblical theology, with its unique focus on historical development and progress, is not best suited for the study of theology proper,"[44] we know what he means (or at least we should). Biblical theology is not best suited for establishing comprehensive doctrinal formulations.[45]

42. See the discussion in Richard C. Barcellos, *The Family Tree of Reformed Biblical Theology: Geerhardus Vos and John Owen—Their Methods of and Contributions to the Articulation of Redemptive History* (Owensboro, KY: RBAP, 2010), 109–35.

43. Vos, *Biblical Theology*, 15–16.

44. James E. Dolezal, *All that is in God: Evangelical Theology and the Challenge of Classical Christian Theism* (Grand Rapids: Reformation Heritage Books, 2017), xv.

45. For a recent brief but helpful discussion on the differences between biblical and systematic theology see J. V. Fesko, *The Spirit of the Age: The 19th-Century Debate over*

We Need Help

And finally, if we are going to retrieve a theological method that serves the church well, we need help. Many in our day were not trained to do theology in a historically Christian manner. (On a personal note, in the past, I often found myself counting texts using a concordance and not weighing their importance in light of their meaning given the entirety of Scripture. I had no concept of distributed doctrines, for example, and their importance for interpretation. This severely hampered my ability to account properly for the *ad extra* operations of the Trinity. At one point in my own experience as a student of Scripture, in terms of theological method, I had to start over.) Because of deficient training, many today need help. For such help, the book by Michael Allen and Scott R. Swain, *Reformed Catholicity: The Promise of Retrieval for Theology and Biblical Interpretation*[46] is recommended as a primer. This book will help you sort through the importance of, and give you a method for, the constructing and accounting of Christian doctrine in a Christian manner. Two more recent books that will help tremendously are Craig A. Carter's *Interpreting Scripture with the Great Tradition: Recovering the Genius of Premodern Exegesis*[47] and Gavin Ortlund's *Theological Retrieval for Evangelicals: Why We Need Our Past to Have a Future.*[48]

---

the Holy Spirit and the Westminster Confession (Grand Rapids: Reformation Heritage Books, 2017), 109–11.

46. Michael Allen and Scott R. Swain. *Reformed Catholicity: The Promise of Retrieval for Theology and Biblical Interpretation* (Grand Rapids: Baker Academic, 2015).

47. Craig A. Carter, *Interpreting Scripture with the Great Tradition: Recovering the Genius of Premodern Exegesis* (Grand Rapids: Baker Academic, 2018).

48. Gavin Ortlund, *Theological Retrieval for Evangelicals: Why We Need Our Past to Have a Future* (Wheaton, IL: Crossway, 2019).

3

Relevant Issues

THIS CHAPTER WILL FOCUS a bit more on the language of the confession. We will consider the relevant issues of 4.1, following the outline of 2LCF below. The General Statement concerning Creation—2LCF 4.1

1. Its inception—2LCF 4.1a; *In the beginning*

2. Its ground—2LCF 4.1b; *it pleased*

3. Its author—2LCF 4.1c; *God the Father, Son, and Holy Spirit*

4. Its goal—2LCF 4.1d; *for the manifestation of the glory of His eternal power, wisdom, and goodness*

5. Its essence—2LCF 4.1e; *to create or make*

6. Its scope—2LCF 4.1f; *the world, and all things therein, whether visible or invisible*

7. Its duration—2LCF 4.1g; *in the space of six days*

8. Its nature—2LCF 4.1h; *and all very good.*

A discussion of most of the points of the outline above will be conducted, though very briefly on some of them. The last four points will be discussed under one heading. This is due to the scope of the book.

THE INCEPTION OF CREATION

The language of WCF, SD, and 2LCF is not uniform at confession 4.1. Though the doctrine confessed is substantially the same, there are some minor differences in form. The differences will be pointed out and discussed as we work our way through the paragraph.

The initial prepositional phrase in 2LCF, "In the beginning," is surely an echo of scriptural language. It is an indication of the inception of creation. Genesis 1:1 says, "In the beginning, God created the heavens and the earth." Poole's commentary on Genesis 1:1 displays that this verse was understood as the inception of creation in the general time-frame of the confession. He says:

> *In the beginning*, to wit, of time and things, in the first place, before things were distinguished and perfected in manner hereafter expressed. Or the sense is this, The beginning of the world was thus. And this phrase further informeth us, that the world, and all things in it had a beginning, and was not from eternity, as some philosophers dreamed.[1]

The Genesis text tells us that God created "the heavens and the earth." This is a broad statement inclusive of everything made. Douglas F. Kelly comments:

> Heavens and earth is a way of saying 'everything that exists', whether galaxies, nebulae or solar systems; all things from the farthest reaches of outer space to the smallest grain of sand or bacterial microbe on planet earth; absolutely everything was created by God. . . .'All things' include the various ranks of angels, and every form of life from whales and elephants to [nonpathogenic] viruses. . . .every form of energy and matter; the speed of light, nuclear structure, electromagnetism and gravity, and all the laws by which nature operates.[2]

A theological paraphrase of Genesis 1:1 could read as follows: "In the beginning, all that is in God brought forth that which is not God." This entails that the entirety of what is external to God is contingent and dependent upon God.[3] The beginning refers to that external work of the eternal God

---

1. Poole, *A Commentary on the Whole Bible*, 1.

2. Douglas F. Kelly, *Creation and Change: Genesis 1.1–2.4 in the Light of Changing Scientific Paradigms* (Geanies House, Fearn, Ross-shire, Scotland, UK: Mentor, 1997, re. 2010), 45.

3. Thanks to Paul Helm who helped purify my thinking in private correspondence on the contingency *and* dependence of creatures.

(who remains as such), effecting the creation of all things, inclusive of time and space. In the seventeenth century, William Ames said, "Time coexists with all created things, as appears in the phrase, *In the beginning*, for that was the beginning of time."[4] Ames continues:

> Place also coexists with things, i.e., the space in which the extension of the creature is defined, Gen. 1:2. But time and place are not, strictly speaking, created but are concreated or connected with created things.[5]

Both time and space, according to Ames, are created with other created things. This should be obvious to us since both time and space are finite, limited, measurable. Herman Bavinck sounds very similar to Ames. He says:

> [I]t is certain, also to human thought, that the world had a beginning and was created in time. Augustine correctly stated that the world was not made in time but along with time, as Plato and Philo and Tertullian had already said before him, and as all theologians since have repeated. . . . Time is the necessary form of the existence of the finite. It is not a separate creation but something automatically given with the world, cocreated with it like space. . . . All change, then, occurs in it, not in God. The world is subject to time, that is, change. It is constantly becoming, in contrast with God, who is an eternal and unchangeable being.[6]

This means that time (as well as space) is creature. Dolezal's comments are helpful with reference to time indicating the measure of creaturely movement.

> Properly considered, time is not an entity or an essence but rather is merely a relation between things that change and are liable to change. Time is concreated with all creatures insofar as it is the measure of all their movement. When we speak of time as a realm we do not mean to imply that it is like a container or box in which temporal things exist, rather we denote simply the created order which is populated by beings that are subject to and undergo change and thus are measured temporally.[7]

---

4. William Ames, *The Marrow of Theology*, trans. John Dykstra Eusden (1968; reprint, Grand Rapids: Baker Books, 1997), 1.7.23 (102).

5. Ames, *The Marrow of Theology,*, 1.7.23 (102).

6. Herman Bavinck, *Reformed Dogmatics*, gen. ed. John Bolt, trans. John Vriend (Grand Rapids: Baker Academic, 2004), 2:429, hereafter *RD*.

7. James E. Dolezal, "Eternal Creator of Time," *Journal of the Institute of Reformed Baptist Studies* (2014): 129, n. 7.

An entailment of this is that creation has always been related to God in time and space, since creation, time, and space are concreated creatures. Creation does not exist outside of time and space; nor do time and space exist outside of creation. Time, space, and "the world, and all things therein" are creatures; God is Creator of all.

THE GROUND OR BASIS OF CREATION

The words "it pleased God" (2LCF 4.1b) refer to divine willing, the decree of God. Ephesians 1:11 says that God "works all things after the counsel of His will." Revelation 4:11 says, "Worthy are You, our Lord and our God, to receive glory and honor and power; for You created all things, and because of Your will they existed, and were created." Creation is due to the will of God. It is not necessary to the divine essence, however. God is God the Trinity without creatures and in no absolute sense (or necessary to the divine nature as such) *must* make creatures. Muller states that both the Lutheran and Reformed of the post-Reformation era agreed on the gratuitous nature of creation. He says:

> The Lutheran and Reformed agree in calling the entire work of creation a free act of God resting solely on the goodness of the divine will. That God created is therefore neither an absolute necessity . . . resting on an antecedent cause nor a necessity of nature . . . since God was not bound by his nature to create the world but could have existed without the creation. The Reformed add that creation is a necessity of the consequence . . . since the divine act of creation does result from the eternal and immutable decree of God . . . [8]

This entails that creation is entirely gratuitous, and this fact ought to enhance our worship as we contemplate it. To be is of the essence of God, or necessary to God, but not to creatures. Creatures do not necessarily exist; their existence is contingent, or by "necessity of the consequence." God willed to create, to bring into contingent existence that which did not exist necessarily, which is everything other than God. Creation did not appear due to absolute divine necessity. In other words, there is nothing in God that makes creation absolutely necessary. Louis Berkhof's words are helpful at this juncture. He says:

> The only works of God that are . . . necessary with a necessity resulting from the very nature of God are the *opera ad intra*, the

8. Muller, *Dictionary*, 83–84.

works of the separate persons within the Divine Being: generation, filiation, and procession. To say that creation is a necessary
act of God, is also to declare that it is just as eternal as those
immanent works of God. Whatever necessity may be ascribed
to God's *opera ad extra*, is a necessity conditioned by the divine
decree and the resulting constitution of things. It is necessity dependent on the sovereign will of God, and therefore no necessity
in the absolute sense of the word. The Bible teaches us that God
created all things, according to the counsel of His will, Eph. 1:11;
Rev. 4:11; and that He is self-sufficient and is not dependent on
His creatures in any way, Job 22:2,3; Acts 17:25.[9]

Mascall's words are a good follow-up to Berkhof's.

> No answer, other than the freedom of the divine will, can be
> given either to the question why God should create a world at
> all, or to the question why, if he does create one, it should be this
> one rather than any other.[10]

The creation is predicated upon the divine pleasure, or will, to create,
as mysterious as that is to us. Though some have argued (I think rightly)
that creation is fitting to the divine essence, this does not entail that creation
is absolutely necessary to the divine essence. Creation, we must affirm, is
utterly gratuitous and mysterious. Mascall's words capture the gratuitous,
mysterious, and wondrous work of creation.

> Once, however, we have been led to affirm God's existence, our
> whole perspective changes, and we see that it is not God's exis-
> tence that requires explanation, but the existence of anything
> else. . . . The real miracle is not that God exists but that the world
> does. God—the self-existent, perfect, changeless Being, the Pure
> Act in whom all that supremely *is* is comprised—how could he
> not exist? The self-existent cannot but be; but that he in whom
> nothing is lacking should confer existence on *us*—that is the
> wonder which may well stagger our minds.[11]

It ought to produce great wonder and awe when we contemplate the fact
that creation is unnecessary to God. Once again, Mascall captures this well.

> So far from diminishing the love shown by God in creation,
> the doctrine that creation is unnecessary to God enhances it. It

---

9. Louis Berkhof, *Systematic Theology* (1939, 1941; reprint, Grand Rapids: Wm. B.
Eerdmans Publishing Co., 1986), 130.

10. Mascall, *He Who Is*, 193.

11. Mascall, *He Who Is*, 95.

is precisely because creation can give nothing whatever to God which in any way enhances his beatitude, that creation is an act of entire giving on the part of God. God would not be lonely or bored or idle if we did not exist; his life as Trinity is a life of infinite activity, of inexhaustible fullness. In creating the world he gains nothing for himself; that is why creation is an act of supreme love.[12]

Before an eloquent and soul-stirring statement by John Webster is quoted, let us remember that theology is an intellectual act, a creaturely reflection, the goal of which is worship. We are attempting to grasp what God has revealed to us, a great privilege, and creaturely theology's goal is communion with God through our Lord Jesus Christ and all its entailments. Here is what Webster says:

God requires nothing other than himself. Yet his unoriginate love also originates. Why this should be so, we are incapable of telling, for, though with much consternation we can begin to grasp that it is fitting that God should so act, created intelligence remains stunned by the fact that God has indeed done so. What stuns us—what our intelligence can't get behind or reduce any further—is the outward movement of God's love, God's love under its special aspect of absolute creativity. God's creative love is not the recognition, alteration or ennoblement of an antecedent object beside itself, but the bringing of an object into being, *ex nihilo* generosity by which life is given. By divine love, the 'infinite distance' which 'cannot be crossed' [quoting Aquinas]—the distance between being and nothing—*has* been crossed. The love of God, therefore, has its term primarily in itself but secondarily in the existence of what is other than God, determined by that love for fellowship with him.

Creation is, again, not necessary for God. God's creative love is not 'a love which is needy and in want' and so 'loves in such a way that it is subjected to the things it loves'; God loves not 'out of compulsion of his needs' but 'out of the abundance of his generosity' [quoting Augustine].[13]

If creation were necessary to the divine essence, it would be the divine essence, for that which is necessary to the divine essence is necessary for the divine to be.

It makes sense to us (kind of) that God created, since we know it is his will to do so, due to divine love and goodness. But the divine will is not

12. Mascall, *God Who Is*, 108–09.
13. Webster, *God without Measure*, 1:92–93.

arbitrary, as in capricious or unreasonable. It is not, as Webster says, to be thought of "as a mere spasmodic exercise of divine power . . ."[14] Divine willing "signifies determination to act according to nature."[15] Mascall says, "That creation is eminently congruous with God's nature we may readily admit . . . but that it is in any way necessary to him we must emphatically deny."[16] God does not have to create in order to be God or in order to be enhanced by that which he created, but create he did, and when he does it reflects who he is. This should astound us and promote worship in us. Listen to Psalm 33:6–9.

> By the word of the LORD the heavens were made, And all the host of them by the breath of His mouth. 7 He gathers the waters of the sea together as a heap; He lays up the deep in storehouses. 8 Let all the earth fear the LORD; Let all the inhabitants of the world stand in awe of Him. 9 For He spoke, and it was *done*; He commanded, and it stood fast.

God is happily God without creatures. Creation is an utterly gratuitous divine effect, indicating to us the "supreme generosity in accord with and on the basis of God's eternal love of himself in the processions of Son and Spirit from the Father."[17] As Daniel Treier says, "Creation was not a necessity but rather a free outpouring of the love that characterizes God's own being."[18] God acts for the love of God. Creation makes sense to us (kind of), and it ought to astound us as we contemplate the divine processions behind creation and meditate upon the divine self-sufficiency and love of Father, Son, and Holy Spirit. Though God is happily God without creatures, creatures exist, and they exist "out of the abundance of his generosity."

THE AUTHOR OF CREATION

Notice these words at confession 4.1c: "the Father, Son, and Holy Spirit." This is an explicit confession of trinitarian creation. Since this will be discussed in some detail in a later chapter, the observation will simply be mentioned at this point. Before continuing, however, it is of interest that identifying the author of creation after an explicit trinitarian manner is not novel to the WCF, SD, or 2LCF. The Confession of the Evangelical Church in Germany

14. Webster, *God without Measure*, 1:93.

15. Webster, *God without Measure*, 1:93.

16. Mascall, *God Who Is*, 110–11.

17. Webster, *God without Measure*, 1:93.

18. Daniel J. Treier, *Introducing Evangelical Theology* (Grand Rapids, MI: Baker Academic, 2019), 95.

(1614), in an article entitled "3. Of the Creation," confesses, "We believe and confess that the true God, the Father, Son, and Holy Spirit, created heaven and earth and all things out of nothing."[19]

THE GOAL OF CREATION

Immediately after the explicit confession of the Trinity in creation, the goal, or *telos*, of creation is confessed in these words: "for the manifestation of His eternal power, wisdom, and goodness" (2LCF 4.1d). Notice that creation has a goal, a *telos*. Our triune God created in order to manifest himself to creatures and, we could add, to be known, loved, served, and adored by his rational creatures (i.e., angels and men). That which has been made has been so in order to manifest God to creatures by creatures, whether in themselves or to and by others (WCF/2LCF 2.2). Creatures, or that which has been made, have been made to *manifest* God's "eternal power, wisdom, and goodness" to creatures.

The language of "manifestation" brings us into the arena of divine revelation, the divine economy. Divine revelation constitutes a manifestation of divine perfections via divine effects, though the effects through which divine perfections are manifested are not themselves divine (i.e., they do not constitute God, nor are they some sort of temporal extension of God). We do not confess divine emanation (i.e., that which God creates in some sense is or becomes God). It must always be remembered that creation is not God. We ought also to remember the following, ably stated by Ian McFarland:

> [T]he end of God's acts in creation do not fill any lack in the agent, since whatever emerges from creation has its immediate cause in God and thus can add nothing to what God already is. Thus where we say (paraphrasing the language of the Westminster Shorter Catechism) that the end of creation is to glorify God, the point is not to suggest that creation augments God's glory in any way, since whatever glory creation might give to God comes from God in the first place. What is distinctive about creation is the *way* in which it displays God's glory. God is already, eternally, and unsurpassably glorious in the threefold act of giving that constitutes God's life as Trinity; but in creation God's glory is manifest outside of God's own life in an act of divine giving that brings into existence myriad beings that are not God. And if God's purpose in creating is in this way simply that creatures

19. James T. Dennison, Jr., *Reformed Confessions of the 16th and 17th Centuries in English Translation*, Volume 4, 1600–1693 (Grand Rapids: Reformation Heritage Books, 2014), 57.

should be as the creatures God intends them to be, then [divine direction to creation's proper end] can be understood as the activity by which God brings it about that creatures should flourish.[20]

The goal of creation is the manifestation of God to creatures for their enrichment, not God's.

The manifestation of the glory of God is the goal of creation. What is meant is not that God receives something from creation that alters or changes him. This is confessed in 2LCF 2.2, which says:

> God, having all life, glory, goodness, blessedness, in and of Himself, is alone in and unto Himself all-sufficient, not standing in need of any creature which He hath made, nor deriving any glory from them, but only manifesting His own glory in, by, unto, and upon them; He is the alone fountain of all being, of whom, through whom, and to whom are all things . . .

Creation does not complete God or make him different in any sense. He wills to create in order to make himself known to creatures, to manifest his glory. Creatures come into existence and receive the capacity to either reflect something of God (e.g., inanimate things) or know him (e.g., angels and men), depending on their created capacities (and with reference to redeemed men due to their re-created capacities [i.e., grace]). God created with an end toward himself. As Ames puts it: ". . . all created things naturally tend towards God from whom they came."[21]

Some have objected that this makes God self-serving and devalues creatures as means to an end. However, as Bavinck observes:

> . . . as the perfect good, God can rest in nothing other than himself and cannot be satisfied in anything less than himself. He has no alternative but to seek his own honor. . . . Inasmuch as he is the supreme and only good, perfection itself, it is the highest kind of justice that in all creatures he seeks his own honor.[22]

Creation *soli Deo gloria* enhances creatures; it does not devalue them. As Mascall says, "That the self-sufficient God deigns to be glorified by his entirely dependent creatures, whose service can add nothing to him, is the supreme privilege and honour that God has conferred upon them."[23] Creation enhances rational creatures not only by giving them being but by orienting

---

20. McFarland, *From Nothing*, 152.

21. Ames, *The Marrow of Theology*, I.viii.21 (102).

22. Bavinck, *RD*, 2:434.

23. Mascall, *God Who Is*, 109.

them toward God, and since some rational creatures (e.g., mankind in Adam) rejected this orientation, God acts to restore and elevate them by the work of the Mediator. For what was not attained due to the fall into sin (i.e., eschatological communion with God) is attained for us by Christ and perfected in us by grace (Heb. 2:10).

Others have claimed that if God created with the goal being his own glory, then he needs creation for that end. Bavinck replies ably:

> God . . . never seeks out a creature as if that creature were able to give him something he lacks or could take from him something he possess. He does not seek the creature [as an end in itself], but through the creature he seeks himself. He is and always remains his own end. His striving is always—also in and through his creatures—total self-enjoyment, perfect bliss. The world, accordingly, did not arise from a need in God, from his poverty and lack of bliss, for what he seeks in a creature is not that creature but himself.[24]

God lacks nothing. He gives what we have in order that we might enjoy that and who he is.

Surely these comments echo such biblical texts as Romans 11:36, which says, "For of Him and through Him and to Him *are* all things, to whom *be* glory forever. Amen." The three prepositional phrases are important to note. Charles Hodge provides a helpful, expanded translation, when he says, "By Him all things are; through His power all things are directed and governed; and to Him, as their last end, all things tend."[25] God is the source, originator, or Creator of all things. God is the sustainer and providential ruler of all things. All things redound to his glory. Everything that is, is for him. In Romans 11:35, Paul echoes words from the book of Job. "If you are righteous, what do you give Him? Or what does He receive from your hand?" (Job 35:7) and "Who has preceded Me, that I should pay *him*? Everything under heaven is Mine" (Job 41:11). What can creatures give to God that he lacks or by which he is enriched? The answer is nothing. God is not in need of gaining anything by virtue of the existence of creatures or the acts of creatures. In fact, it is impossible for God to gain or lose anything by virtue of the existence or acts of creatures or even himself.

Though beyond the scope of this book, it is important to note that the ultimate goal of creation, in terms of creaturely experience, is what the older writers called the beatific vision. This is not "a vision of the eye, except with

---

24. Bavinck, *RD*, 2:43; bracketed words are original.

25. Charles Hodge, *Romans* (Reprint 1989; Edinburgh and Carlisle, PA: The Banner of Truth Trust, 1835), 379.

reference to the perception of the glorified Christ. . . . [but is] an inward . . . act of intellect and will."[26] It is ectypal theology without the need of mortification and with the continual, unresisted vivification of the Spirit. It is the theology of the blessed, the theology of vision.[27] It is that for which pilgrims hope. It was secured for us by our Lord. This vision will occur when the saints shall be in "the presence of His glory with exceeding joy" (Jude 24), whatever that means.

THE ESSENCE, SCOPE, DURATION, AND NATURE OF CREATION

Confession 4.1 also asserts the essence, scope, duration, and nature of creation: "to create or make [essence] the world, and all things therein, whether visible or invisible [scope], in the space of six days [duration], and all very good [nature]."

This is where the 2LCF is unique in terms of the major seventeenth-century British confessions. It does not contain the words "of nothing," as do the WCF and the SD. Those confessions read as follows: "It pleased God the Father, Son, and Holy Ghost, for the manifestation of his eternal power, wisdom, and goodness, *in the beginning*, to create or make *out* [SD] *of nothing* [WCF and SD] the world, . . ." (emphasis added). The phrase "in the beginning" is fronted in the 2LCF but not in the other confessions. The phrase "[out; SD] of nothing [WCF and SD]" is not contained in the 2LCF. This phrase is an explicit confession of creation *ex nihilo*, creation of nothing, or creation by God without the use of pre-existing materials.

Ex nihilo refers to the bringing into existence of being that had no being without change in the Being who brought what was not in being into being. God is productive of things but did not first produce things from things. Creation *ex nihilo* has no material cause. Technically speaking, therefore, creation *ex nihilo* is not creation out of God, if one means by that "creation by extension or diffusion."[28] "[E]very creature exists solely because God wants it to exist."[29] *Ex nihilo* does not mean creation from nothing absolutely, for from nothing can come nothing. McFarland, utilizing an analogy from creatures, says:

---

26. Muller, *Dictionary*, 395.

27. See Junius, *A Treatise on True Theology*, 129–33. See also Muller, *Dictionary*, 360.

28. John Webster, "Creation out of Nothing," in *Christian Dogmatics: Reformed Theology for the Church Catholic*, Michael Allen and Scott R. Swain, eds. (Grand Rapids: Baker Academic, 2016), 143.

29. McFarland, *From Nothing*, 186.

> While a potter creates from clay, God does not create from any-thing. In other words, 'nothing' does not identify the substance out of which God brings creatures to be, but rather declares that God's creative act is conditioned by and dependent on nothing other than God alone, who is the sole antecedent condition of any creature's existence.[30]

Creation *ex nihilo* implies the following: "that creation is grounded in *nothing but God*, . . . the existence of *nothing apart from God*, and [that] . . . in creation *nothing limits God*."[31] This, of course, does not mean that God is all there is, for that which is not God exists. It does mean, however, that whatever exists other than God is not God and has come into existence because of God. McFarland states it clearly: "[c]reatures are ontologically distinct from God and yet have no ground of existence other than God."[32] "To be created from nothing is to have the ground and substance of one's being in God, and in God alone."[33] God brings things into being though not from things in being (i.e., creatures). Creation *ex nihilo* is an introduction by God of being different from God. K. Scott Oliphint is correct when he says, "When Christians speak . . . of creation *ex nihilo*, what is actually meant is creation from nothing except God."[34] The English Puritan Thomas Watson offers these humbling words:

> God made the world without any pre-existent matter. This is the difference between generation and creation. In generation there is suitable material at hand, some matter to work upon; but in creation there is no pre-existent matter. God brought all this glorious fabric of the world out of the womb of nothing. Our beginning was of nothing. Some brag of their birth and ancestry; but how little cause have they to boast who came from nothing.[35]

The absence of the phrase "of nothing" in the 2LCF requires us to ask and answer a question. Does its absence mean the 2LCF denies creation *ex*

---

30. Ian F. McFarland, "The Gift of the *Non aliud*: Creation from Nothing as a Metaphysics of Abundance," *International Journal of Systematic Theology*, Volume 21, Number 1, (January 2019): 47.

31. McFarland, *From Nothing*, 87.

32. McFarland, *From Nothing*, 94.

33. McFarland, "The Gift of the *Non aliud*, 54.

34. K. Scott Oliphint, *God with Us: Divine Condescension and the Attributes of God* (Wheaton, IL: Crossway, 2012), 13, n. 11. I take the preposition "from" in Oliphint's statement as a denial of divine emanation, extension, or diffusion.

35. Thomas Watson, *A Body of Divinity: Contained in Sermons upon the Westminster Assembly's Catechism* (Edinburgh and Carlisle, PA: The Banner of Truth Trust, 2000), 116.

nihilo? The answer to this question is no, and here is why. Notice the words "create or make" in 2LCF. These are not necessarily synonymous terms. The word "create" can refer to the production of being or matter and the word "make" can refer to the formation of created matter. This reflects Genesis 2:3, where we read, "Then God blessed the seventh day and sanctified it, because in it He rested from all His work which God had *created* and *made*" (emphasis added). The two terms used here justify the distinction in 2LCF. Poole's commentary on Genesis 2:3 gives evidence that the distinction was observed in the general time-frame of the confession. He says:

> *Which God created and made;* either 1. *Created in making,* i. e. made by way of creation; or rather, 2. Created out of nothing, and afterwards out of that created matter *made* or formed divers things, as the beasts out of the earth, the fishes out of the water. He useth these two words possibly to show that God's wisdom, power, and goodness was manifest, not only in that which he brought out of mere nothing, but also in those things which he wrought out of matter altogether unfit for so great works.[36]

This is what is intended by these terms in the 2LCF. To "create" implies "from nothing" and to "make" means to form from something. Also, there is no comma after "to create or," which most likely indicates that "make" is not synonymous with "to create." It could well be that the framers of the 2LCF considered the phrase "[out] of nothing" to be superfluous. This will be discussed further in the next chapter. It will be argued that this distinction between "to create" and "make" is contained in the theological literature behind the 2LCF and is an appropriate distinction to confess.

The confession asserts that our triune God was pleased "to create or make [essence], the world . . . [scope], in the space of six days [duration], and all very good [nature]." Creation is of a different order of being from the Creator. Creation includes everything not God. The initial act of creation identified by the confession occurred "in the space of six days." The nature of created things via their creation was "very good."[37]

---

36. Poole, *A Commentary on the Whole Bible*, 5.

37. The somewhat abrupt ending to this chapter is due to the scope of the book. For a treatment of the phrase "in the space of six days," I highly recommend the lecture by Dr. James M. Renihan. It can be found here: https://www.sermonaudio.com/sermon-info.asp?SID=1120171359450.

4

What is Creation?

JOHN WEBSTER ASSERTS:

> [T]he starting-point for a Christian doctrine of creation, as
> for any Christian doctrine, is God in himself (theology, says
> Bonaventure, 'begins at the very beginning, which is the first
> principle'). Only out of the sheer antecedent perfection of God's
> life *in se* can we feel the force of the concept of creation.[1]

In order to define what creation is, we must know something of the Creator.
This will be further displayed in the discussion below.

This chapter provides a working definition of creation and reflects on
four seventeenth-century definitions. This survey provides the necessary
background for the following chapter, which interacts with the views of
two contemporary theologians. The following chapter argues that the views
proposed by these two authors depart from the manner in which Reformed
theologians have historically upheld the Creator/creature distinction (and
other related issues), which is vital for the entire theological enterprise.

---

1. Webster, *God without Measure*, 1:88.

A WORKING DEFINITION OF CREATION

What is creation? Quite often, when asked that question, everyday Christians would immediately direct attention to what has been made. One might say, "Look at the vast sky above, with its moon and stars, its sun and clouds which give rain from heaven." We might point to the ocean and all its deep mysteries or the Grand Canyon's majestic scenery. This is not a wrong answer to the question. Theologians of the Christian theological tradition, however, give a more theocentric answer to that question. This is certainly due to the fact that they are theologians. But if we ponder the question a bit more, contemplating how the Bible presents to us the account of creation in Genesis 1, our answer would start with God and go out from there. For example, when defining the work of creation, Bavinck says, "[Creation is] that act of God through which, by his sovereign will, he brought the entire world out of nonbeing into being that is distinct from his own being."[2] Notice that Bavinck begins his definition in a theocentric manner. Creation is an act of God, accomplished through his sovereign will. Bavinck's definition is important for it clearly upholds a Creator/creature distinction. Creation is of another order of being from divine being. Mascall rightly asserts, "[God] is outside and above the order of the universe and is radically different in status from all the beings that compose it."[3] Created being is *brought into existence* by God; divine being *is*. There are two orders of being—created being and non-created, or divine, being. The former is finite (i.e., having bounds or limits according to its created capacities); the latter infinite (i.e., having no bounds or limits according to its uncreated essence and is thus incomprehensible to the creature). The former is temporal (i.e., it began-to-be with time and exists in relation to it); the latter eternal (i.e., ever existing, "without beginning or end and apart from all succession and change"[4]). The former is dependent; the latter independent. Creatures are contingent; God is not. As John of Damascus said long ago, "All things are distant from God . . . by nature."[5] Created nature and divine nature are *both* distinct *and* different in kind.

Bringing things into being distinct from himself makes God the efficient cause of creation. That is, God, and God alone, the triune God, brought creation into existence *without any change in God the Trinity*. According

---

2. Bavinck, *RD*, 2:416.
3. Mascall, *He Who Is*, 115.
4. Muller, *Dictionary*, 18.
5. As quoted in McFarland, *From Nothing*, 59.

to Edward Feser, "An efficient cause is that which brings something into existence."[6] Feser adds elsewhere:

> An efficient cause . . . is that which brings something into being . . . An efficient cause thus actualizes a potency, and it does so by exercising its own active potencies or powers.[7]

With reference to God, this means that, since he is pure act, or not becoming or able to become in any sense, he alone is able to bring about the existence of things without change in himself. In fact, change in God is impossible. Divine existence is not one of "incomplete realization," as Muller puts it.[8] God is "the fully actualized being, the only being not in potency . . . "[9] Muller continues:

> . . . God in himself, considered essentially or personally, is not *in potentia* because the divine essence and persons are eternally perfect, and the inward life of the Godhead is eternally complete and fully realized.[10]

God does not possess some sort of potency, some latent potential, to become what he is not. Nothing can change God; not creation nor even God himself. The execution of divine power, then, does not make God what he is not; it reveals or manifests who he is.

Creation is a work of God, bringing being into being "distinct from his own being," as Bavinck says. The Creator is of a different order of being from the creation; God is not like us. This distinction is crucial to maintain. As Thomas Weinandy says, "As Creator, God . . . is not one of the things created, and is thus completely other than all else that exists."[11] Webster's penetrating words are to the point:

> The difference between creator and creature is infinite, not just 'very great'; 'creator' does not merely refer to the supreme

---

6. Edward Feser, *Scholastic Metaphysics: A Contemporary Introduction* (Piscataway, NJ: Translation Books Rutgers University, 2014), 88.

7. Feser, *Scholastic Metaphysics*, 42.

8. Muller *Dictionary*, 11.

9. Muller *Dictionary*, 11.

10. Muller, *Dictionary*, 11. Muller goes on to state the following: "This view of God as fully actualized being lies at the heart of the scholastic exposition of the doctrine of divine immutability . . . Immutability does not indicate inactivity or unrelatedness, but the fulfillment of being."

11. Thomas Weinandy, "Human Suffering and the Impassibility of God," *Testamentum Imperium* Volume 2, 2009: 1. This can be found on-line at http://www.preciousheart.net/ti/2009/52-. Accessed 9 February 2015.

causal power by which the world is explained, for God would then be simply a 'principle superior to the world,' or 'the biggest thing around.' Such conceptions falter by making God one term in a relation, and so only comparatively, not absolutely, different. . . . God the creator is not simply the most excellent of beings, because the distinction between uncreated and created being is not a distinction *within* created being but one between orders of being; God is not one item in a totality, even the most eminently powerful item in the set of all things.[12]

Confessing divine simplicity, eternity, infinity, immutability, and impassibility (WCF/2LCF 2.1) means that God cannot change from within or from without because of what he is and what he is not. He is God, the simple and immutable Creator; he is not in any sense a mutable creature, nor does he become one, in the sense of changing divine being. He is, according to Muller, "free from all mutation of being, attributes, place, or will . . ."[13] He can and does reveal who he is to creatures, but he does not refashion himself or add attributes, or perfections, to do so. By creating, God does not become something he was not in order to reveal who he is; he simply reveals who he is by creation, providence, and grace. As Duby says:

God does not change in relation to the creature. Instead, the creature changes in relation to him without any change in the God who is already immanently determinate in his own plentitude and whose eternal decretive act wisely encloses all the travails of redemptive history.[14]

The relationship creatures have with him does not necessitate the creation and assumption of relational properties (as some in our day claim which will be discussed later), though it does necessitate the use of analogical, relational language (in the case of Scripture) to and for us indicating that he is near.

DEFINITIONS OF CREATION BY FOUR SEVENTEENTH-CENTURY REFORMED THEOLOGIANS

We will now consider how some theologians defined creation in the general time-frame of the confession. The next chapter will interact with two

12. Webster, *God without Measure*, 1:91.

13. Muller *Dictionary*, 162.

14. Steven J. Duby, *Divine Simplicity: A Dogmatic Account* (London, New York, Oxford, New Delhi, Sydney: T&T Clark, 2016), 144, 145.

contemporary authors who assert things not reflected in the older Reformed writers. In order for this to become clear to readers, it is vital to pay close attention to what the older writers both affirm and what they deny, either explicitly or implicitly.

Johannes Wollebius

In the early seventeenth century, Johannes Wollebius defines creation as "the act by which God made the world and all that is in it, partly from nothing and partly from unsuitable material, in order to reveal the glory of his power, wisdom, and goodness."[15] Notice two things in this definition. First, Wollebius distinguishes between creation "partly from nothing" and "partly from unsuitable material." He goes on to explain himself as follows: "To create means not only to make something out of nothing, but also to make something beyond the power of nature, from unsuitable material."[16] He gives an example of what he means by "unsuitable material" in these words: "there was no quality or disposition in the dust that would have produced the human body, which was formed unnaturally and miraculously from it."[17] His point is that the first human body was not created out of nothing immediately, and that from which it was formed had nothing in it from the act of creation *ex nihilo* that tended toward some sort of natural formation of man. This makes the evolution of man from matter untenable, according to Wollebius. He implicitly denies evolution at this point. The dust of the ground was formed into the body of man by a creative act of God (Gen. 2:7), not by virtue of a natural process, the seeds of which were formerly infused into the dust.

The second thing to be noted is where Wollebius says God created "in order to reveal the glory of his power, wisdom, and goodness." This triad is in the confession at 4.1. Wollebius uses the same triad at least two other times in the context of discussing creation.[18] This shows that the triad was not invented *de novo* by the Westminster Divines.[19]

15. Johannes Wollebius, "Compendium Theologiae Christianae," in *Reformed Dogmatics*, Edited and Tranlated by John W. Beardslee III (Grand Rapids: Baker Book House, 1977), 54.

16. Wollebius, "Compendium Theologiae Christianae," 54.

17. Wollebius, "Compendium Theologiae Christianae," 54.

18. Cf. Wollebius, "Compendium Theologiae Christianae," 50 and 56.

19. Wollebius' "Compendium Theologiae Christianae" was first published in 1626, two decades prior to the WCF. The triad, "power, wisdom, and goodness" occurs in The Bohemian Confession (1535). "Hence they [i.e., Scripture, Nicaea, and "the Confession or Symbol of Athanasius"] teach the supreme power, wisdom, and goodness of

William Ames

William Ames defines creation as follows: "Creation is the efficiency [or working power; see p. 91] of God whereby in the beginning out of nothing he made the world to be altogether good."[20] He further asserts that "[c]reation refers to the whole world, i.e., whatever exists outside of God."[21] Defining the world as "whatever exists outside of God" gives us a glimpse into what is meant by "world" in confession 4.1 (i.e., all that is not God). The use of "world" as referring to the created realm is clearly echoed in Scripture itself. Psalm 90:2 says, "Before the mountains were brought forth, Or ever You had formed the earth and the world, Even from everlasting to everlasting, You *are* God" and Acts 17:24 says, "God, who made the world and everything in it, since He is Lord of heaven and earth, does not dwell in temples made with hands." In good classical and orthodox Christian fashion, Ames then says, "Nothing exists from eternity but God, and God is not matter or a part of any creature, but only the maker."[22]

Ames distinguishes between created matter and form. He says, ". . . all things which exist outside of God are created—fully created, that is, in matter as well as in form."[23] "Some things are said to be created whose matter preexisted . . ."[24] The best example of this is man. Man was formed

---

this one and the same God . . ." James T. Dennison, Jr., *Reformed Confessions of the 16th and 17th Centuries in English Translation*, Volume 1, 1523–1552 (Grand Rapids: Reformation Heritage Books, 2008), 303. The Forty-Two Articles of the Church of England (1552/53) also utilize this triad. "There is but one living, and true God: and He is everlasting: without body, parts, or passions: of infinite power, wisdom, and goodness . . ." Dennison, *Reformed Confessions*, 2:2. The Thirty-Nine Articles (1562/63) contain the same triad. See Dennison, *Reformed Confessions*, 2:754. The Irish Articles of 1615 also contains these terms. "There is but one living and true God, everlasting, without body, parts, or passions, of infinite power, wisdom, and goodness; the Maker and Preserver of all things, both visible and invisible. And in unity of this Godhead there are three persons of one and the same substance, power, and eternity, the Father, the Son, and the Holy Ghost." Dennison, *Reformed Confessions*, 4:92. This triad in the context of trinitarian creation will be discussed in a later chapter. The three terms, "wisdom, power, goodness" occur together in The Second Confession of the London-Amsterdam Church of 1596 (also known as the 1596 True Confession), though not in the context of discussing trinitarian creation. See James T. Dennison, Jr., *Reformed Confessions of the 16th and 17th Centuries in English Translation*, Volume 3, 1567–1599 (Grand Rapids: Reformation Heritage Books, 2012), 749. These three terms also show up in The Formula Consensus Helvetica (1675). See Dennison, *Reformed Confessions*, 3:522.

20. Ames, *The Marrow of Theology*, I.viii.2 (100).
21. Ames, *The Marrow of Theology*, I.viii.5 (100).
22. Ames, *The Marrow of Theology*, I.viii.9 (101).
23. Ames, *The Marrow of Theology*, I.viii.6 (100).
24. Ames, *The Marrow of Theology*, I.viii.10 (101).

from pre-existing, created matter, "the dust of the ground" (Gen. 2:7). Francis Turretin makes a similar distinction. The creation of man, according to Turretin, is called mediate creation.[25] By "mediate" Turretin means that "which is made indeed from some matter."[26] Immediate creation is creation *ex nihilo simpliciter* (i.e., simply, directly, straightforwardly, in and by itself [e.g., Gen. 1:1]). The material being of man, however, comes from creation *ex nihilo* but not immediately or directly by the *ex nihilo* act of divine power. It is, most likely, the distinction between immediate and mediate creation that is reflected in the 2LCF in the words "to create or make." This is probably why "[out] of nothing" was not included. Some things were made from other things; not all things were made by the initial divine *ex nihilo* act.

Francis Turretin

Moving from Ames's discussion of creation to Turretin's gives us more background of the discussions around the general time-frame of the confession. He begins his discussion of creation with these words: "We intend now to speak of the transient and external acts (called the works of God) by which he executes his decrees outside of himself."[27] Turretin then distinguishes between the works of nature and grace; nature referring to creatures and their natural ends and grace referring to men and their supernatural ends.[28] The works of nature are two-fold: creation and providence. Turretin says, "The first work of nature is creation, by which he formed out of nothing as to its whole being this entire universe and all that is in it."[29] In good Turretinian fashion he goes on to make distinctions. "Creation may be either first and immediate (which is simply *ex nihilo*) or secondary and mediate (which is made indeed from some matter)."[30] In other words, there are created things, then some things made or formed from those previously created things. Again, man is a fitting example.

Turretin goes on to say that

---

25. See Francis Turretin, *Institutes of Elenctic Theology*, 3 vols., ed. James T. Dennison, Jr., trans. George Musgrave Giger (Phillipsburg, NJ: P&R Publishing, 1992–97), V.1.6 (1:432).

26. Turretin, *Institutes*, V.1.6 (1:432). Gill makes the same distinction in the eighteenth century. See Gill, *A Body of Doctrinal and Practical Divinity*, 256–57.

27. Turretin, *Institutes*, V.1.1 (1:431).

28. Turretin, *Institutes*, V.1.1 (1:431).

29. Turretin, *Institutes*, V.1.3 (1:431).

30. Turretin, *Institutes*, V.1.6 (1:432).

there is no change made in God by [creation]. Nor is any new perfection added to him . . . Hence whatever change was made by the creation was made in the creatures passing from nonexistence to being and not in God himself creating.[31]

This is standard language among older Reformed theologians when distinguishing between God and not God, or all that is God and all that is not God.

Herman Witsius

Witsius defines creation as follows: "Creation is that act of God, in which, by the all-powerful command of his will, he made out of nothing, and perfected, the whole universe, in the space of six days."[32] He distinguishes between immediate and mediate creation while advocating creation *ex nihilo*.

If we consider the first origin of things, all of them were created of nothing. Some, however, were made immediately of nothing, as the first works of the first day, and all spiritual substances: others, mediately, as the works of the subsequent days, which indeed were made of matter; but of matter that in itself was ill adapted to the purpose, that bore no resemblance to the things produced from it, and from which no such creatures could have been produced by any natural energy.[33]

The most admirable circumstance in creation is, that, at the mere command of the Deity, all things rose into existence either out of nothing, or out of matter which was altogether inadequate, and bore no proportion to what was to be formed from it.[34]

Witsius views time as having a beginning. Commenting on the first verse of the Bible he says:

---

31. Turretin, *Institutes*, V.1.12 (1:433). Though I understand what Turretin is seeking to communicate, technically speaking, creatures do not pass from nonexistence to being. The initial act of creation does not change creatures; it brings into being that which was not. Non-existent patients (i.e., creatures) cannot be the objects upon which God operates, causing them to pass "from nonexistence to being." It is impossible for God to be the agent acting upon nonexistent "things."

32. Herman Witsius, *Sacred Dissertations of the Apostle's Creed*, Volume 1 (1823; reprint, Grand Rapids, Reformation Heritage Books, 2010) 181. These words by Witsius are capitalized in the original.

33. Witsius, *Sacred Dissertations*, 1:194.

34. Witsius, *Sacred Dissertations*, 1:196.

It is said, "In the beginning God created the heaven and the earth;"—which intimates that the beginning of time, by which the duration of all created things is circumscribed, coincided with the creation of the world.[35]

The account of creation by Witsius is similar to the others surveyed above. Creation is an act of God which has come about due to the will of God. Some things were brought into existence *ex nihilo* (including time) and others were made from the existing matter brought into being by God.

Before drawing a brief conclusion to this survey, recall these words of Turretin: "Nor is any new perfection added to him . . ." Neither creatures nor God change God by virtue of creation *ex nihilo*. No "new perfection [is] added to him."

CONCLUSION

This brief survey can help us understand the intent of confession 4.1. It can also supply us with a background with which we can compare the views of contemporary writers. The comparison of these older theological statements about creation with the views of two contemporary writers is the concern of the next chapter.

35. Witsius, *Sacred Dissertations*, 1:205.

5

Change in God Given Creation?

Is IT CONSISTENT WITH God's being to claim some sort of change in God due to creation? Does creation bring with it a manner of difference in God's existence? Does God add anything to himself in order to create and/or manifest himself to creatures? A statement made by Ames (quoted in the previous chapter) is of interest in our day due to the fact that some have attempted to assert and distinguish between divine modes of existence given creation. Note what Ames says: "Nothing exists from eternity but God, and God is not matter or a part of any creature, but only the maker."[1] God is "only the maker" and in no sense part of that which is made. If he were part of that which is made, God would change from being eternal to being (at least partly) temporal, from being infinite to being (at least partly) finite, from being simple to being (at least partly) composed, from being immutable to being (at least partly) mutable. Focusing more on denying change in God due to creation, Turretin (also quoted in the previous chapter) says:

> there is no change made in God by [creation]. Nor is any new perfection added to him . . . Hence whatever change was made

---

1. Ames, *The Marrow of Theology*, I.viii.9 (101).

by the creation was made in the creatures passing from nonexistence to being and not in God himself creating.[2]

Similarly, Wilhemus à Brakel says, "[The] creative act does not bring about a change in God but in the creature."[3] The statements by Ames, Turretin, and à Brakel are reflective of the way older theologians spoke about the distinction between God and creatures. In God there is no change, given creation or not. In terms of his being and essence, his existence and attributes, God does not go *from* and *to* in any sense. Given creation or not, God just is God the Trinity. He does not become more or less divine or relatable. He does not add divine features to himself. Instead, we ought to affirm with Thomas Weinandy that "God as God and God as Creator are one and the same."[4]

The views of two contemporary writers who have articulated themselves in a different manner from Ames, Turretin, and à Brakel will now be considered. In fact, it will be contended that their proposals steer away from the classical Christian and confessional Reformed position. The views of these two writers were chosen due to their connection to the confession and their influence upon others by the publication of their many books. Before stating and critiquing their views, however, it may be helpful to remind ourselves that *ideas* are being critiqued not *individuals*, *proposals* not *people*. While doing so, attacking the character of those with whom disagreement is lodged is not in view whatsoever. The particular views critiqued below, which have been advocated in print in more than one place, it will be argued, are wrong. The views to be examined are not in-step with the theological tradition of their authors. The catholic and Reformed traditions get it right, it will be argued, and anyone who currently holds these views needs to seriously reconsider them.

---

2. Turretin, *Institutes*, V.1.12 (1:433). See n. 31 in the previous chapter for qualification of this statement.

3. Wilhelmus à Brakel, *The Christian's Reasonable Service*, Volume I (Grand Rapids: Reformation Heritage Books, 1992, Third printing 1999), 99. To be precise, creation does not bring about a change in creatures. Creatures do not exist prior to being created. They do not and cannot undergo change via the creative act of God because that which does not exist cannot change. "Before" creation came into being, there was no change nor time, the measure of creaturely change, nor "at the point of" creation was there change in terms of some thing or things going from and to.

4. Thomas Weinandy, *Does God Change?: The Word's Becoming in the Incarnation* (Still River, MA: St. Bede's Publications, 1985), 183.

JOHN FRAME: "TWO MODES OF EXISTENCE IN GOD"

The first contemporary theologian that will be considered is John Frame. Frame says, "My approach . . . recognizes *two modes of existence* in God . . ."[5] Previous to this statement he says, "The *difference* between God's atemporal and historical *existences begins*, not with the creation of man, but with creation itself."[6] Let us consider these words: "*two modes of existence* in God" and "The *difference* between God's atemporal and historical *existences begins* . . . with creation itself." Does this proposal work? It certainly does not comport with the claims of Ames, Turretin, and à Brakel above, as will be demonstrated.

Frame posits two modes of divine existence. He claims explicitly "*difference* between God's atemporal and historical *existences*" and that this difference "*begins* . . . with creation." This seems to entail a difference between God's essence and existence. While discussing divine essence and existence, seventeenth-century theologian Francis Cheynell says the following:

> We must not conceive that God was first in a *naked Power* of Being, and afterwards reduced [i.e., changed] unto *actual Being* by his own *effectual Power* as if his existence were really different from his essence, as its proper cause.[7]

More will be said about this issue below. For now, remember that Frame claims at least one of God's modes of existence *began* and it is *different from* his other mode of existence: one is "atemporal" and the other is "historical." This entails that in some sense God's existence is "really different from his essence," as Cheynell says above. Frame claims a "*difference* between God's atemporal and historical *existences begins* . . . with creation itself." The historical mode of existence must be a derived existence, since it is not eternal, which entails something as derivatively divine in God due to creation. A feature in God came-to-be in God given creation. Is this not a contradiction? This must be the case since God's historical existence began and must be, therefore, part of creation prior to man's existence. If God's so-called historical existence began with creation, it cannot be God's atemporal existence. God's historical existence, therefore, came-to-be, but to come-to-be is a necessary and exclusive feature of creatures. According to Geerhardus

---

5. John M. Frame, *The Doctrine of God* (Phillipsburg, NJ: P&R Publishing, 2002), 572; emphasis added.

6. Frame, *Doctrine of God*, 571; emphasis added.

7. Francis Cheynell, *The Divine Trinunity of the Father, Son, and Holy Spirit* (London: Printed by T. R. and E. M. for Samuel Gellibrand at the Ball in Pauls Church yard, 1650), 8; emphasis original, spelling modernized.

Vos, "That cannot be."[8] Frame's view is that God came to possess a second mode of divine existence which began-to-be with creation. According to this view, God was, in fact, "reduced unto *actual Being* by his own *effectual Power* . . .," in the words of Cheynell above. Assuming this to be the case, Vos's "That cannot be" applies to Frame's proposal as will become evident below when the Vos statement is considered in context. Frame's proposal is not reflective of the confessional Reformed position.

Frame makes other assertions which are not reflective of the Reformed theological tradition. For example: ". . . relenting belongs to God's very nature . . . Relenting is a divine attribute. . . . relenting is part of God's unchangeable divine nature."[9] Just how relenting can be "part of God's unchangeable nature" is not explained with any degree of cogency. Relenting implies changeableness not unchangeableness.[10]

8. Geerhardus Vos, *Reformed Dogmatics, Volume One: Theology Proper* (Bellingham, WA: Lexham Press, 2012–2014), 5. Someone might attempt to refute this, claiming Vos is not speaking of God's historical existence but his atemporal existence. Vos, as far as I can tell, however, never speaks of God's historical existence as Frame does.

9. John M. Frame, *Systematic Theology: An Introduction to Christian Belief* (Phillipsburg, NJ: P&R Publishing, 2013), 370. For a review article of Frame's *Systematic Theology* see Ryan M. McGraw, "Toward a Biblical, Catholic, and Reformed Theology: An Assessment of John Frame's *Systematic Theology: An Introduction to Christian Belief*," in *Puritan Reformed Journal*, 8, 2, (2016): 197–211. McGraw points out several departures from more traditional discussions of various Christian doctrines. For example, McGraw says: "Much more could be said about Frame's *Systematic Theology* that illustrates where he suffers from a paucity of historical theology, such as shifting from discussing God's intent in the free offer of the gospel to something approximating English hypothetical universalism; misunderstanding the historical context of the lapsarian controversy; importing the two natures of Christ into pre-incarnate theophanies; careless language on the Trinity, such as referring to "three divine beings"; inadequate understanding of the relationship between eternal generation and aseity in Reformed theology; imputing to the Son "eternal obedience" and even "eternal subordination of role" in relation to the Father; importing Christ's threefold office into the definition of the image of God, rather than describing man's function in the world in terms of these offices; opening the door for those who say that Adam was the head of a pre-existing group of early hominids, rather than existing by the special creation of God; redefining the Reformed doctrine of total depravity and accusing the traditional doctrine as teaching that man is as bad as he can be; questioning the legitimacy of a logical order in the traditional *ordo salutis*; and urging the church to adopt elements of Presbyterianism, Congregationalism, and Episcopalianism simultaneously and at its own discretion" (McGraw, "Toward a Biblical, Catholic, and Reformed Theology," 211; for each claim, McGraw cites page numbers for Frame's book).

10. For helpful discussions on divine relenting from both exegetical and theological bases, see Baines, et al., *Confessing the Impossible God*, 75, 90, 91, 96, 97, 125, 130, 157, 158, 159, 160, and 166. In Frame's *Salvation belongs to the Lord: An Introduction to Systematic Theology* (Phillipsburg, NJ: P&R Publishing, 2006), 29, he says: "The Bible teaches that God has all the emotions we have, though in a more perfect way. . . . Some say that because

K. SCOTT OLIPHINT: GOD "DECIDES TO BE SOMETHING ELSE AS WELL"

Another example of a contemporary author who argues for a change in God's existence due to creation is K. Scott Oliphint.[11] In his *God with Us* he contends "that God freely determined to take on attributes, characteristics, and properties that he did not have, and would not have, *without creation*."[12] Earlier in Oliphint's discussion he tells us that "attributes," "properties," and even "perfections" are used synonymously.[13] It seems that he uses "characteristics" in the same sense (see the discussion below). God does this *taking on* in order to relate to man both prior to the incarnation of the Son and even "for eternity." Oliphint asserts:

> He remains who he is, but *decides to be* [emphasis added] something else as well; he decides to be the God of the covenant. It was, to be sure, a monumental decision. It changed the *mode* of God's existence for eternity; *he began to exist* [emphasis added] according to relationships *ad extra*, which had not been the case before.[14]

Note what Oliphint claims: "the *mode* of God's existence" changed "for eternity." How so? An act of God, based on a decision of God, changed God forever; that is, God changed God. God willed a change of mode in divine existence.[15] Oliphint says, ". . . he *began to exist* [emphasis added] according

---

of God's self-sufficiency he cannot suffer. That is called *impassibility*. Certainly, God cannot suffer any loss of his attributes or divine nature, but the grief we spoke about earlier is certainly a kind of suffering" (emphasis original). Later Frame says: "God can't suffer, man can suffer. . . . God, who cannot suffer, has taken to himself a human nature, in which he can suffer, in Christ" (130). Can God suffer or not? Is God impassible or not? The WCF, SD, and 2LCF assert that God is "without passions" (2.1). Granted, in the latter statement Frame locates suffering "in Christ" but the way he states himself is not precise enough to distinguish between the acts of the Mediator who works according to both natures "by each nature doing that which is proper to itself" (WCF, SD, 2LCF 8.7). Frame says: "[God] can suffer, in Christ." It is much better to say the Son of God incarnate suffered according to his human nature. God, as God, cannot suffer. Putting it this way preserves divine impassibility and upholds the revealed mystery of the distinct acts of our two-natured Mediator. Maybe this is what Frame intends by his words. If so, there are better ways to state oneself.

11. See footnote 4 in chapter 1.

12. Oliphint, *God with Us*, 110; emphasis added.

13. Oliphint, *God with Us*, 13.

14. Oliphint, *God with Us*, 254–55, emphasis original.

15. It could be that what Oliphint intended is that God willed and effected a change in modes of divine *revelation*. If that is what is meant, it is not clear and could have been stated better. A change in modes of divine revelation is one thing; a change in modes of divine existence is quite another.

to relationships *ad extra* . . ." How can God remain who he is but become "something else as well" without some sort of addition in or to God? He cannot. If God becomes "something else as well," would this not entail some sort of composition in God? It seems it would, thus compromising divine simplicity (i.e., God is not composed of parts).[16]

Listen to à Brakel as he speaks to this very issue:

> Since we must recognize, however, that all composition implies imperfection, dependency, and divisibility, we may not think of God as being composite even in the remotest sense of the word.[17]

God cannot come-to-be in any sense. He cannot become "something else as well." To become "something else as well" would entail some sort of divine composition. But Oliphint tells us that "he began to exist . . ."? Creatures begin to exist; God is. Creatures are related to God by God; God is. Oliphint posits that God took to himself new perfections. Would this not compromise divine simplicity, infinity, eternity, and immutability? Instead, it must be affirmed that the change brought about by creation does not entail change in God's existence.[18]

A RESPONSE TO THE PROPOSALS OF FRAME AND OLIPHINT

How should one respond to these proposals? Very carefully, indeed; but a response is necessary if for no other reason than these proposals are quite at odds with the long-held view that God's existence (i.e., *that* he is) and God's

16. See Jeffrey C. Waddington, "Something So Simple I Shouldn't Have to Say It." Available at https://reformedforum.org/something-so-simple-i-shouldnt-have-to-say-it/. Accessed 15 February 2020. Waddington argues that there are "two senses in which divine simplicity is denied" by Oliphint. He says, "Dr. Oliphint seems to believe he maintains biblical and Reformed orthodoxy by maintaining the *mere* existence of God's essential nature. But in this schema, there are two senses in which divine simplicity is denied in fact even if not in intention. First, the *very distinction* between God's essential nature and his covenantal nature, brought about by the assumption of covenantal properties or attributes is itself a contravention of the doctrine of divine simplicity. Second, the covenantal nature is itself changeable or mutable, not to say malleable. To sum up my concerns, Dr. Oliphint has *ontologized* in his theological formulation what has been understood by the vast majority of the Christian tradition as a *relation* between the absolutely immutable Creator and his changeable creatures."

17. à Brakel, *The Christian's Reasonable Service*, 1:96.

18. It could be that what Oliphint intended by the words "he began to exist" is that creation is related to God given its existence. If that is so, it is not clear and could have been stated better.

essence (i.e., *what* he is) are coextensive. The fact that God is (i.e., his exis-tence [*esse*; to be or the act of existing]) and that which God is (i.e., *essentia*; essence, the whatness or quiddity of someone or thing), though they *may be* distinguished conceptually *must never be* separated really. Muller defines the essence of God as follows:

> essentia Dei: *the essence or "whatness" of God;* God is the only necessary, self-existent being or, in other words, the only being in whom *esse* (q.v.), or existence, and *essentia* (q.v.), or essence, are inseparable; it is of the essence or "whatness" of God that God exist.[19]

Note these words well: "God is the only . . . being in whom . . . existence . . . and . . . essence . . . are inseparable . . ." This, according to Muller, is reflective of the position of Protestant Scholastic theology, and certainly reflected in the WCF, SD, and 2LCF. God does not take on new divine being; in fact, he does not "have" being, as if being were something without God added to him to make him to be who and what he is. God just is his being. Cheynell says, "We must not conceive . . . as if his existence were really different from his essence, or did virtually flow from, and consequently depend upon his essence, as its proper cause."[20] There cannot be a consequent aspect of God's existence dependent upon his essence, or upon anything else (e.g., decree, creation).

In the late nineteenth century, Geerhardus Vos said:

> There is no distinction in God between essence and existing, between essence and being, between essence and substance, between substance and its attributes. God is *most pure* and *most simple* act.[21]

Vos then poses this question: "*May we make a distinction in God between His being and His attributes?*"[22] Here is his answer:

> No . . . If His attributes were something other than His revealed being, it would follow that also essential deity must be ascribed to His being, and thus a distinction would be established in God between what is essentially divine and what is derivatively di-vine. That cannot be.[23]

19. Muller, *Dictionary*, 110.
20. Cheynell, *The Divine Trinunity*, 8.
21. Vos, *Reformed Dogmatics*, 1:5.
22. Vos, *Reformed Dogmatics*, 1:5; emphasis original.
23. Vos, *Reformed Dogmatics*, 1:5.

Some context will be provided for this statement then an explanation will be offered. Earlier in his discussion, Vos says, "Now there is nothing higher than God, and God is simple, without composition."[24] It is important to keep this in mind while trying to understand what Vos means in the quote above. God is without composition. He is simple. He cannot be added to or subtracted from because he just is. All additions or subtractions imply composition (or decomposition). Now, when Vos says, "If His attributes were something other than His revealed being," he is distinguishing between, for argument's sake, God in himself without revelation (i.e., "His attributes") and God revealed to us (i.e., "His revealed being"). Then when he says, "it would follow that also essential deity must be ascribed to His being," he is referring to, for sake of argument again, God's *revealed* being. It could be paraphrased this way: "If God's eternal attributes without creation were something different from his revealed being with creation, it would follow that also essential deity must be ascribed to his *revealed* being."

If this is the case, and it seems to be the only way to make sense of Vos's assertion, then it makes sense of his next words: "and thus a distinction would be established in God between what is essentially divine and what is derivatively divine. That cannot be." Vos's point is that given divine simplicity, an ontological distinction cannot be established between what is essentially God and what God reveals himself to be. There is no such thing as derivative deity. God comes-to-be in no sense whatsoever. There are not varying existences in God, one of which is not co-extensive with the very essence of God. In other words, Vos would disagree with Frame's proposal (as well as Oliphint's), utilizing the doctrine of divine simplicity and the co-extensive concepts of divine existence and essence.[25] Vos's statements cannot be harmonized with Frame's or Oliphint's views; they are incompatible.

These proposals entail that all that is in God is not God eternally; or it could be put this way, some feature in God is not God eternally. Frame and Oliphint, though perhaps inadvertently, end up both distinguishing and separating divine essence from divine existence. Contrary to this, God does not begin-to-be in any sense whatsoever. Divine existence and essence are co-extensive; and God's existence does not "flow from, and consequently depend upon his essence, as its proper cause," as Cheynell says. God does not cause any feature of his existence to come-to-be, but if his so-called historical existence or Oliphint's condescended mode of existence (see below)

24. Vos, *Reformed Dogmatics*, 1:5.

25. Someone might claim that Frame and Oliphint are not using the word "exist" in a technical sense and that I am requiring a degree of precision in terms and concepts beyond their intent. When theologians speak of God, however, they owe the Christian world precision and they ought to use terms with their common, established meanings.

are real and if either came-to-be with creation, then they were caused-to-be with creation, and that cannot be. In fact, as Duby asserts, ". . . God by his own nature already contains all that might be required for his action in creation."[26]

Stephen Charnock's words may help sort through the issues at this point. He says:

> He is from himself;[27] not that he once was not, but because he hath not his existence from another, and therefore of necessity he did exist from all eternity. . . . [God is] what he is from eternity, and cannot be otherwise; and is not what he is by will, but by nature, necessarily existing, and always existing without any capacity or possibility ever not to be.[28]

> . . . God being infinitely simple, hath nothing in himself which is not himself, and therefore cannot will any change in himself, he being his own essence and existence.[29]

> Though God alway remains in regard of existence, he would be immortal and live alway; yet if he should suffer any change, he could not properly be eternal, because he would not alway be the same, and would not in every part be eternal; for all change is finished in time, one moment preceding, another moment following; but that which is before time cannot be changed by time. God cannot be eternally what he was; that is, he cannot have a true eternity, if he had a new knowledge, a new purpose, a new essence; if he were sometimes this and sometimes that, sometimes know this and sometimes know that, sometimes purpose this and afterwards hath a new purpose; he would be partly temporary and partly eternal, not truly and universally eternal. He that hath anything of newness, hath not properly and truly an entire eternity.[30]

Both *that* God is and *what* God is he is eternally and by nature. God does not will himself to come-to-be. God is not his own cause, though he is the alone sufficient ground of his existence. Divine existence is not caused-to-be. God

---

26. Duby, *Divine Simplicity*, 146.

27. I prefer "of" instead of "from."

28. Stephen Charnock, *The Existence and Attributes of God*, two volumes (reprint, from the 1853 edition by Robert Carter & Brothers; Grand Rapids: Baker Book House Company, 1979, Eighth printing, February 1988), 1:51.

29. Charnock, *Existence and Attributes*, 1:333.

30. Charnock, *Existence and Attributes*, 1:333.

is not his own efficient cause. He exists, and in no sense comes-to-be. As à Brakel says, "the essence of God is His eternal self-existence."[31] Berkhof is correct when he says:

> God is self-existent, that is, He has the ground of His existence in Himself. This idea is sometimes expressed by saying that He is *causa sui* (His own cause), but this expression is hardly accurate, since God is the uncaused, who exists by the necessity of His own Being, and therefore necessarily [and, I would add, "and eternally"].[32]

God's existence (i.e., that he is) and essence (i.e., what he is) are coextensive. Though these concepts may be distinguished logically for pedagogical purposes, they must never be viewed as separate—as if one followed upon the other. Duby's comments are worthy of our affirmation when he says:

> . . . if God's existence were objectively distinct from his essence, it would be caused either by God's essence or by an external principle or agent. But it cannot be caused by God's essence, for this would entail that God would cause himself to be. Nor can it be caused by another, for, according to God's aseity in Holy Scripture, God receives nothing from another, least of all his very existence.[33]

God does not effect or affect God. If God possesses a second mode of existence (i.e., his historical mode) or a singular mode which he changed in order to create and/or relate to that which he creates (i.e., his condescended mode), then the second mode was caused-to-be or the singular though willed to-be-changed mode was caused-to-be. This entails some sort of chronology within God's being. Listen to à Brakel again: "There can be no chronology within the Being of God since His Being is simple and immutable."[34] Divine simplicity and divine immutability (and eternity and infinity) defy chronology in God. Bavinck's words are to the point:

> Indeed, the idea of becoming predicated of the divine being is of no help in theology. Not only does Scripture testify that in God there is no variation nor shadow due to change [James 1:17], but reflection on this matter also leads to the same conclusion. Becoming presupposes a cause, for there is no becoming without

31. à Brakel, *The Christian's Reasonable Service*, 1:88.
32. Berkhof, *Systematic Theology*, 58.
33. Duby, *Divine Simplicity*, 125.
34. à Brakel, *The Christian's Reasonable Service*, 1:92.

a cause. But being in an absolute sense no longer permits the inquiry concerning a cause. Absolute being is because it is. The idea of God itself implies immutability. Neither increase nor diminution is conceivable with respect to God. He cannot change for better or worse, for he is the absolute, the complete, the true being. Becoming is an attribute of creatures, a form of change in space and time.[35]

The claim is made by Oliphint, however, that God changed his mode of existence "for eternity." This is something God decided to become. Oliphint pushes his view of divine condescension back of creation to the decree. He says:

> The condescension begins before 'the beginning.' Covenantal condescension did not have its genesis in Genesis. It did not begin in history. It began in eternity-past. . . .That decree was itself condescension.[36]

God's covenantal condescension occurred, his changed mode of existence came about due to the divine decree and given creation, as with Frame. Because of creation (and God's desire to relate to it covenantally), God *takes on* that which he had not prior to creation. This means that these attributes, these characteristics, properties, and perfections are themselves created, something Oliphint affirms. He says:

> So, there can be little question, as one reads of the varying appearances[37] of Yahweh throughout covenant history that, in order to appear at all, Yahweh takes on created properties and characteristics. He condescends to present himself, and in doing so he takes characteristics and attributes that belong to creation.[38]

---

35. Bavinck, *RD*, 2:158.

36. K. Scott Oliphint, *The Majesty of Mystery: Celebrating the Glory of an Incomprehensible God* (Bellingham, WA: Lexham Press, 2016), 117.

37. Yahweh is not appearing, as if he was not present then became present. He is omnipresent and infinite. Appearances, or theophanies, are revelational; they reveal what is. They do not entail new reality, features, or being in God. They entail new revelation for creatures to ponder (i.e., ectypal knowledge). Attempting to read Oliphint charitably, it seems to me that it would be much better if he said "Yahweh utilizes created things to reveal himself, to communicate knowledge to the creature, but in no sense does this entail any ontological or accidental addition in God." The addition is not God, though revelatory of God (see the discussion below). Oliphint's proposal seems to view theophanies as entailing the acquisition of mediatorial actuality, or intermediary divine being.

38. Oliphint, *God with Us*, 209; see also 13, n. 8, 198, and 208. If Oliphint simply means that God condescends to reveal himself by using revelational modalities

A fundamental problem with these proposals (i.e., Frame's and Oliphint's) involves the Creator/creature distinction. In an effort to account for divine immanence, Oliphint's proposal entails that God, revealing himself to creatures, cannot be *both* transcendent *and* immanent so must become something (prior to the incarnation of the Son) he was not (prior to the creation of all things). God acts in this new manner of existence in order to reveal himself to and interact with us "for eternity." This assumes a problem with divine transcendence (and infinity; see below), if God is going to reveal himself to creatures. In fact, according to Porter, Oliphint as much admits this. Here is what Porter says:

> Repeating a particular formula of "in order to" and "so that he could" when articulating his conception of divine condescension, Oliphint suggests there is a "problem . . . of the distance of God" which God needs to voluntarily overcome because it "constitutes a boundary between the being of God and the being of creation" (97). Whether necessitated or assumed freely (Oliphint affirms the latter), this amounts to God having another manner in which he exists—an acquired mode of being that affords him the ontological conditions by which he can interact with his creation. Contrary to Oliphint's assertions, the "answer" to the question of how this transcendent God can be in true and relational immanence is not found in the taking on of ontological newness "in order to relate," but in the fact that God is able to relate *because of who he is ontologically* (without the need of intermediary actuality).[39]

Is Porter correct in his analysis? It surely seems so and here is why. In the book Porter is referring to by Oliphint, *The Majesty of Mystery: Celebrating the Glory of an Incomprehensible God*, we find statements like this:

> There is, then, a distance of being between God and man. How can the Infinite One relate to finite creatures?[40]

> [There is a] problem (for us, not for God) of the distance of God, which distance constitutes a boundary between the being of God and the being of creation.[41]

---

belonging to creation, there are better ways of stating such.

39. Porter, "*The Majesty of Mystery*," 89–90.
40. Oliphint, *The Majesty of Mystery*, 95.
41. Oliphint, *The Majesty of Mystery*, 97.

> The problem of distance and the dilemma of God's relationship to creation is no problem or dilemma for Him.[42]

The reason why "the problem of distance" is not a problem for God is found in God. For, in the words of Oliphint, "the absolute and the relative exist, first and foremost, in the Triune God Himself!"[43] By "absolute" Oliphint intends what God is essentially or "God's characteristics *as God* (and, thus, quite apart from creation)."[44] He lists among these characteristics God's infinity, eternity, immutability, and impassibility.[45] What he intends by "relative" is "[t]he characteristics that God has because of His voluntary condescension . . ."[46] He also labels these as God's covenantal characteristics.[47] He says, "Some of those [relative/covenantal] characteristics are now permanent (e.g., grace, wrath), some only temporary (e.g., theophanies, human forms, appearances as fire, in the Old Testament)."[48] So the "distance of being between God and man" is bridged by God himself. God remains infinite, eternal, immutable, and impassible in his essential characteristics, but he also must be viewed as "expressing Himself in 'new' characteristics in order to relate to us."[49] And both God's absolute and relative character exist in God. Recall these words of Oliphint: "the absolute and the relative exist, first and foremost, in the Triune God Himself!"[50]

It appears that Oliphint is using a somewhat traditional distinction when he uses the terms "absolute" and "relative." For example, John Owen says:

> The properties of God are either *absolute* or *relative*. The absolute properties of God are such as may be considered without the supposition of any thing whatever, towards which their energy and efficacy should be exerted. His relative are such as, in their

42. Oliphint, *The Majesty of Mystery*, 101.

43. Oliphint, *The Majesty of Mystery*, 103.

44. Oliphint, *The Majesty of Mystery*, 102.

45. See Oliphint, *The Majesty of Mystery*, 102.

46. Oliphint, *The Majesty of Mystery*, 102.

47. See Oliphint, *The Majesty of Mystery*, 102.

48. Oliphint, *The Majesty of Mystery*, 105.

49. Oliphint, *The Majesty of Mystery*, 101. It seems that Oliphint has changed the way he states his covenantal properties/characteristics proposal in this book. In *God with Us* he uses the language of God taking "on attributes, characteristics, and properties" (110). In *The Majesty of Mystery* he uses "expressing Himself" (101) and "the covenantal characteristics . . . are expressed by God" (103), for example.

50. Oliphint, *The Majesty of Mystery*, 103.

> egress and exercise, respect some things in the creatures, *though*
> *they naturally and eternally reside in God* [emphases added].[51]

Note well, however, Owen's final words: "though they naturally and eternally reside in God." What Owen identifies as relative properties "naturally
and eternally reside in God." Oliphint suggests to readers that God's relative
characteristics are either permanent or "only temporary (e.g., theophanies,
human forms, appearances as fire, in the Old Testament)." Just how God's
relative characteristics such as these mentioned by Oliphint can be both
temporary and "naturally and eternally reside in God" is not clear.

A case can be made that Owen and Oliphint use the terms absolute
and relative differently. If relative perfections "naturally and eternally reside
in God," as Owen contends, how can some of them be temporary, finite,
here one day and gone tomorrow, as Oliphint's proposal entails? This needs
to be explored in more detail.

Owen explains the distinction between absolute and relative properties in God. He says:

> Of the first sort [i.e., absolute] is God's immensity ; it is an abso-
> lute property of his nature and being. For God to be immense,
> infinite, unbounded, unlimited, is as necessary to him as to be
> God ; that is, it is of his essential perfection so to be. The ubiq-
> uity of God, or his presence to all things and persons, is a rela-
> tive property of God ; for to say that God is present in and to all
> things supposes those things to be. Indeed, *the ubiquity of God*
> *is the habitude of his immensity to the creation*.[52]

Ubiquity is a creaturely predication of God given creation. It "naturally
and eternally" resides in God, however, indicating his immensity. Owen
continues:

> Supposing the creatures, the world that is, God is by reason
> of his immensity indistant to them all ; or if more worlds be
> supposed (as all things possible to the power of God without
> any absurdity may be supposed), on the same account as he is
> omnipresent in reference to the present world, he would be so to
> them and all that is in them.[53]

Owen views relative properties as those attributed to him by creatures
given creation. When creatures affirm God's omnipresence, for example,

51. John Owen, *The Works of John Owen*, 23 vols., ed. William H. Goold (Edinburgh; Carlisle, PA: The Banner of Truth Trust, 1982 edition), 12:93.

52. Owen, *Works*, 12:93; emphasis added.

53. Owen, *Works*, 12:93.

it is an attempt to recognize and account for divine immensity given that creatures exist. Omnipresence is not something added to God given the world of creatures; it is how we affirm divine immensity as we relate to God. Relative properties do not entail some new feature in God or new features added (or subtracted) by God in order to create and/or relate to creatures. As Duby puts it, "[God] does not — indeed need not — undergo processes of development for the sake of his providential oversight."[54] Relative divine attributes "are simply modulations of the already actual perfections of power and love without the entailment of divine development."[55]

The relative attributes do not accrue to God for to accrue involves a happening to and an addition. Accruing relative attributes would entail accidents in God. Oliphint's proposal seems to entail both.[56] Whether that is the case or not, it is important to deny any accrual or accidents in God whatsoever. Duby's comments help with these very issues.

> The absolute attributes 'belong to God from eternity and without respect of creatures' [quoting Polanus], while the relative 'belong to God in time with some relation toward creatures' [quoting Aquinas]. The former are identical to God's essence considered absolutely (though still under diverse aspects), while the latter are identical to God's essence considered in relation to the creature under some aspect or creaturely circumstance. God does not undergo change so as to accrue the relative attributes as accidents; rather, the creature undergoes change, taking up a new relation to God and thus meeting the same divine essence in new ways. For example, the absolute attribute of love is not enlarged to include mercy; rather, the creature enters a pitiable state and then begins to encounter the love of God as mercy.[57]

If Oliphint's relative divine characteristics are not infinite, eternal, immutable, and impassible as the absolute, this entails they are finite, temporal, mutable, and passible, unless there is some third option which is impossible to conceive. In his book *God with Us*, Oliphint actually says, "there must be some real and fundamental sense in which God *can* have or experience

---

54. Duby, *Divine Simplicity*, 147.

55. Duby, *Divine Simplicity*, 147.

56. See James E. Dolezal, "Objections to K. Scott Oliphint's Covenantal Properties Thesis." Available at http://www.reformation21.org/articles/objections-to-k-scott-oliphints-covenantal-properties-thesis.php. Accessed 5 January 2018. Doelzal suggests that "Oliphint understands the covenantal properties to be real existing attributes that accrue to God . . ." (n. 5).

57. Duby, *Divine Simplicity*, 205.

passions."[58] But if the relative really exists "in the Triune God Himself," then, in the words of Porter, God must have assumed "an acquired mode of being that affords him the ontological conditions by which he can interact with his creation," and thus, the boundary or "distance of being" has been bridged. The answer to Oliphint's question "How can the Infinite One relate to finite creatures?" seems to be that he assumes finitude in himself. "He remains who he is, but decides to be something else as well," in the words of Oliphint.

If Oliphint can assert "there must be some real and fundamental sense in which God *can* have or experience passions" based on his covenantal properties proposal, could not this be extended further to other "'new' characteristics"? For example, given the covenantal properties proposal, one might posit the following: "there must be some real and fundamental sense in which God *can*" be finite, temporal, mutable, and/or composed. Oliphint argues the following in *God with Us*: ". . . one of the covenantal properties that he takes to himself is the development of knowledge"[59] and ". . . the lack of knowledge that God has, as given to us in Genesis 22:12, is a covenantal lack . . ."[60] He argues similarly from Genesis 3:9, "Then the LORD God called to Adam and said to him, 'Where *are* you?'" He says, "In condescending to relate to Adam and Eve, he is, like them (not essentially, but covenantally) restricted in his knowledge of where they might be hiding in that garden."[61] So, according to this theory, "there must be some real and fundamental sense in which God *can*" be ignorant and, therefore, not omniscient. Oliphint further claims that "God takes on covenant characteristics that are consistent with his essential character."[62] Though he attempts to balance this statement with the acknowledgement that some "covenant characteristics . . . seem to us to be inconsistent with that character"[63] (i.e., God's essential character), it is hard to fathom how a covenantal lack of knowledge can be consistent with divine omniscience, for example.[64]

---

58. Oliphint, *God with Us*, 87, emphasis original. See my interaction with Oliphint on the issue of divine impassibility in Richard C. Barcellos, "The New Testament on the Doctrine of Divine Impassibility (II)," in *Confessing the Impassible God*, 208ff.

59. Oliphint, *God with Us*, 194.

60. Oliphint, *God with Us*, 195. For interaction with Oliphint's proposal on Gen. 22, see Steve Garrick, James P. Butler, and Charles J. Rennie, "The Old Testament on Divine Impassibility," in *Confessing the Impassible God*, 147–50.

61. Oliphint, *God with Us*, 111.

62. Oliphint, *God with Us*, 228.

63. Oliphint, *God with Us*, 228.

64. The two final sentences of this paragraph come from Richard C. Barcellos, "The New Testament on the Doctrine of Divine Impassibility (II)," in *Confessing the Impassible God*, 205.

This thesis assumes an ontological problem that must be overcome. Oliphint says, there is "a boundary between the *being* of God and the being of creation" (emphasis added). But is there such a problem or boundary? Obviously, there is an ontological difference, but does this entail a relational boundary? McFarland asserts there is no "sort of ontological barrier that might limit God's intimacy with creation."[65] Duby says, "God . . . has no gap to bridge in order to draw near to us, and in fact we can only exist where he is: 'in him we live and move and have our being' (Acts 17:28)."[66] Weinandy says, "The Persons of the Trinity being fully actualized relations contain no potency which needs to be actualized or overcome through new actions in order to establish new relations."[67] And Bavinck says, "Implied in creation is both God's transcendence and God's immanence . . ."[68] Genesis 1:1 says, "In the beginning God created the heavens and the earth." Psalm 75:1 says, "We give thanks to You, O God, we give thanks! For Your wondrous works declare *that* Your name is near." The works of God are revelatory of the fact that he *is* near. God need not overcome God in himself to become God with us.

Both Frame and Oliphint assume a working tenet of aspects of what some call theistic personalism or mutualism; namely, given classical Christian theism, there are ontological features in the eternal God which must be overcome if divine immanence is to be. Frame even admits the following: "My approach bears a superficial resemblance to process theology, which also recognizes two modes of existence in God, transcendent and immanent . . ."[69] Frame assumes something to be true as asserted by process (and open) theists without questioning it. Charles J. Rennie addresses this issue with reference to Oliphint.

> In *God with Us*, K. Scott Oliphint proposes a novel solution to a theological problem that has been posed by modern liberals and open theists. As is too often the case, the older tradition is dismissed and the presuppositions of the liberals are granted without argument. Early in the book, in an argument against an opposing view, Oliphint states, "One of the questions that should be asked in this regard is why the orthodox tradition did not see the need to posit such things" (77). This is precisely the question Oliphint should have asked the open theists, and we must now ironically ask of Oliphint. Why should it be taken for granted

65. McFarland, *From Nothing*, 55.

66. Duby, *God in Himself*, 227.

67. Weinandy, *Does God Change?*, 185.

68. Bavinck, *RD*, 2:110.

69. Frame, *Systematic Theology*, 378.

that there is a problem that needs to be solved? Why didn't the orthodox tradition see the need to posit created covenantal properties of God apart from the actual incarnation? Wouldn't a closer examination of the Reformed tradition suggest that much of the contemporary debate assumes a false dilemma between God's transcendence and immanence? Can we even assume that they were asking the same questions? And if not, why not?[70]

The same applies to Frame.

Transcendence and immanence, however, are not "two modes of existence in God." Transcendence is a creaturely affirmation of the otherness of divine being given creation. Immanence is a creaturely affirmation of divine presence given creation. Process theism sees "a fundamental metaphysical continuity between God and all that is not God."[71] Frame and Oliphint deny this, and rightly so. Both, however, posit a need for God to overcome something in him in order to create and/or relate to creatures. Instead, as Duby says, ". . . God's freedom from spatial confinement is also his positive capacity for unrestricted nearness to all creatures in all places."[72] Treier's words echo Duby's where he says, "Transcendence and immanence are not pure opposites, despite what humans might suppose. God is so transcendent as to be immanent to anyone and everyone simultaneously."[73]

Process theism further asserts that "[o]nly if God and the world operate on the same metaphysical plane is it possible for God to engage the world both directly and without compulsion."[74] Is God, in fact, an ontological boundary or barrier which must be overcome if he is to reveal himself to creatures? Is it the case that there is "a boundary between the *being* of God and the being of creation" (emphasis added), which functions like an ontological chasm that must be crossed via some sort of change in or addition to God if he is to reveal himself to creatures? The answer is no. In fact, asserting that there is such a boundary and that God has overcome it by his will infuses a dialectic into one's theology proper which wreaks havoc upon it. McFarland is surely correct when he asserts, "God's engagement with the world is neither impeded by nor subject to the metaphysics of becoming."[75]

---

70. Rennie, "Appendix I," in *Confessing the Impassible God*, 408.

71. McFarland, *From Nothing*, 18.

72. Duby, *Divine Simplicity*, 152.

73. Treier, *Introducing Evangelical Theology*, 95. See Treier's discussion on omnipresence, transcendence, and immanence on p. 111.

74. McFarland, *From Nothing*, 18.

75. McFarland, *From Nothing*, 19.

God does not become in order to create or manifest himself to creatures. Creation manifests the eternal God to creatures. McFarland continues:

> For while God's acting outside of God's self to bring into being that which is other than God does not involve any blurring of the distinction between God and the creature, neither does it presuppose any sort of ontological barrier that might limit God's intimacy with creation.[76]

If God pleases to manifest himself to creatures, then God does so; and he is so pleased. This is stated at confession 4.1. Again, the God confessed as manifesting himself at 4.1 is the same God confessed in chapters 2 and 3.

There is another problem with Oliphint's proposal. His view of God condescended and God as infinite and eternal seem to be two orders of being—one temporal and contingent (i.e., created or derived, even though willed-to-be) and the other eternal and non-contingent (i.e., uncreated). The condescended mode of existence comes about due to a boundary between God and creatures. The boundary is God himself. Recall what Oliphint says, "There is a boundary between the being of God and the being of creation." How does God overcome the "problem of the distance of God"? He condescends. "He remains who he is, but decides to be something else as well."[77] What gets revealed to us in order to overcome this boundary is the condescended, covenantal mode of being, a mode of being not co-extensive with who God is eternally, a mode of being that is not simple, not infinite, not eternal, not immutable, not impassible, and not omniscient. The older Reformed writers did not speak in this manner at all, nor does the confession allow such talk of God. God has no newly-produced attributes; indeed, God has no produced attributes whatsoever. Instead, "there is no change made in God by [creation]. Nor is any new perfection added to him . . ."[78] As Duby assures us:

> . . . when God acts in the life of his creatures, he is not acting by something added to his own being or by changing from who he is *in se* [i.e., in himself] to who he is *pro nobis* [i.e., for us]. He does not have to develop himself in any way in order to meet us in the economy. He simply exercises outwardly what he himself is as God in accomplishing his good works in our midst. We therefore never encounter a secondary iteration of God but rather only the one true God himself freely turned toward us in his holiness and love. Perhaps unexpectedly, then, the old inflection of God's

76. McFarland, *From Nothing*, 55.
77. Oliphint, *God with Us*, 254.
78. Turretin, *Institutes*, V.1.12 (1:433).

aseity as pure actuality serves to corroborate and emphasize that God is fully himself in all his activity *ad extra*.[79]

In *The Majesty of Mystery* Oliphint uses the terms "character" or "characteristics" instead of the more conventional "attribute" or "attributes" on numerous occasions. He identifies what he calls God's essential characteristics and his relative or covenantal characteristics.[80] That character and characteristics function like attribute and attributes normally function seems to be the case from these words of Oliphint:

> In the history of theology, there have been various ways to attempt to categorize God's characteristics. Some have said that God has some characteristics that are *incommunicable* and some that are *communicable*. . . .
>
> Other categories that have been proposed to distinguish God's characteristics are "metaphysical and moral" characteristics, or "absolute and relative."[81]

Oliphint's condescended/relative characteristics are derived and contingent. This entails that they are created, which would mean that God has become, in some sense, part creature. In response to Oliphint's covenantal properties proposal, Dolezal says:

> They appear to be contingent, caused, and dependent on God's free will for their existence. In sum, the covenantal properties seem to be creaturely rather than divine. If they were divine attributes then we would now have to speak about features of divinity that are temporal, finite, contingent, caused and dependent. This is exactly the opposite of what divinity is. The covenantal properties seem plainly not to be eternal, infinite, necessary, or any of the other things we normally ascribe to God's attributes. It is perhaps, then, not an exaggeration to conclude that for Oliphint God *as covenantal* is a creature and not divine.[82]

79. Duby, *God in Himself*, 223.

80. See Oliphint, *The Majesty of Mystery*, 102–03.

81. Oliphint, *The Majesty of Mystery*, 101. At the end of the paragraph quoted above, he adds these words: "All of these categories can be helpful in explaining the differences in God's perfections." Here "perfections" is used instead of attributes or characteristics.

82. Dolezal, "Objections to K. Scott Oliphint's Covenantal Properties Thesis." In a book review of Oliphint's *God with Us*, Charles J. Rennie provides similar critique to the covenantal properties thesis. See Rennie, "Appendix I," in *Confessing the Impassible God*, 399–408.

It is much better to say, as Ames did, "God is not matter or a part of any creature, but only the maker"; and, it could be added, he is not made in any sense whatsoever.

God not only does not but cannot change his mode of existence or add a second one (i.e., a different mode of divine being). The various modalities of revelation (i.e., creation, conservation, re-creation, consummation), we must affirm, constitute no change in God either. His works do not make him to-be. The change is in creatures, such as effects derived from divine operation, which include words written or spoken by prophets, apostles, and our Lord. The God who reveals himself to creatures remains God as he is without creatures. The varying modalities of divine revelation constitute no change in God, but they do constitute change in the creature. Divine revelatory acts (e.g., creation) do not in any sense constitute, compose, or establish the being of God; they reveal, or manifest, who he is. It is certain that the acts of God reveal God to us (though not exhaustively or comprehensively) and though the revelatory modalities are not God, they are means through which it is just God who is revealed to us as he who is immanent. Divine immanence does not come about due to change in the divine. It is revealed with the stuff of creation and throughout the economy. Duby's words are to the point:

> . . . if God is complete in himself and is not determined at all by reference to a counterpart, he transcends the world in a manner that robustly facilitates his immanence. . . . He is free to live and act among his creatures in the economy without in any way altering himself to "fit in" or qualifying his presence in order to avoid being assimilated to the world.[83]

Again, Scripture is clear—divine transcendence is not a boundary to be overcome in order for God to be immanent. "For thus says the High and Lofty One Who inhabits eternity, whose name *is* Holy: 'I dwell in the high and holy *place*, With him *who* has a contrite and humble spirit, To revive the spirit of the humble, And to revive the heart of the contrite ones'" (Isa. 57:15).

Modes of divine revelation and modes of divine existence (or orders of divine being) are not the same thing. Modes of revelation do not constitute a second-level divine existence which becomes determinative of divine action. Oliphint argues this when he says, "he takes on characteristics that *determine* just how he will interact with us . . ."[84] The transcendent is immanent to creation, however, and he tells us so via revelational modalities;

83. Duby, *God in Himself*, 225.
84. Oliphint, *God with Us*, 12; emphasis added.

and though the modalities are themselves revelational of the divine nature and persons, they are not constitutive of either, nor are these determinative of divine action. God's transcendence is not a problem to be overcome by the taking on of new characteristics which subsequently determine his actions. Concerning divine transcendence and immanence, it can be put in this manner: God is transcendent because he is God, or divine. We could say the same thing about divine immanence: God is immanent because he is God, or infinite. He does not, however, become immanent via self-induced ontological, accidental, creaturely, new additions of any sort. He does not tinker with himself in order to reveal himself. Both God's transcendence and immanence are perfections relative to creatures which are revealed to us, but neither entails divine mingling with creatures. As Vos says, "Even where God's immanence comes to the fore, God and the world still remain unmixed."[85] According to the Bible and the confession, God—Father, Son, and Holy Spirit—manifests himself via creation, conservation, re-creation, and consummation. Note well *that* he manifests (i.e., reveals) and note well *what* he manifests (i.e., himself; his "eternal power, wisdom, and goodness"). Revelation is God's telling creatures that he *is* with us; it is not the divine *becoming* with or for us. God does not change God in order to become present with us; he causes us to come into being and changes us. Again, modes of divine revelation and modes of divine existence are not the same thing.

WHAT DRIVES THESE PROPOSALS?

It appears that both Frame and Oliphint attempt the same thing. They try to account for divine immanence with creatures, given divine transcendence. To do this, they both posit some sort of divine change, that God relates himself to creatures by adding to or acting upon himself. In some sense, God is the effect of his own will and action, a partly self-decreed and actuated being, both a first and a second cause.[86] But as Webster assures us, "God's simplicity excludes any relation to creatures in which God receives an augmentation of his being . . ."[87] God does not augment God to be God with us. He brings creatures into being and augments them to reveal that he is near. The proposals by Frame and Oliphint (though unintentionally) end

---

85. Vos, *Reformed Dogmatics*, 1:165. Vos's comment is in the context of discussing Gen. 1:2, "And the Spirit of God was hovering over the face of the waters." Immediately prior to the statement referenced above, he says, "But the Spirit of God hovers on and above the waters. He does not mingle with them" (165).

86. I owe the essence of this sentence to Cameron G. Porter.

87. Webster, *God without Measure*, 1:126.

up compromising *both* divine simplicity *and* divine immutability, as well as divine infinity and divine eternity.

Another motivation for these proposals is to account for what has traditionally been termed metaphorical language, and specifically the anthropomorphic and, especially, anthropopathic scriptural assertions predicated of God. This is certainly commendable. Both Frame and Oliphint, however, view the traditional manner of explaining these metaphorical predications as wrong and in need of reform. For example, Frame says:

> Theologians have sometimes described God's relenting as "anthropomorphic." There is some truth in that description . . .
>
> But the historical process does change, and as an agent in history, God himself changes. On Monday, he wants something to happen, and on Tuesday, something else. He is grieved one day, pleased the next. In my view, *anthropomorphic* is too weak a description of these narratives. In these accounts, God is not merely *like* an agent in time. He really *is* in time, changing as others change. And we should not say that his atemporal, changeless existence is more real than his changing existence in time, as the term *anthropomorphic* suggests. Both are real.[88]

God's "changeless existence" and "his changing existence in time . . . are real"? Both exist? This claim sounds very similar to the view of Karl Rahner as asserted by Joseph Donceel, quoted by Weinandy. "Accordingly, 'Rahner seems to distinguish two aspects in God: God as he is in himself and God as he is in the otherness of world history. He is immutable in the first aspect, he really changes in the other one.'"[89] Frame's position does not account properly for the metaphorical language of Holy Scripture and sounds dangerously like some form of process theism.

Contrast the words of Frame quoted above with those of Vos, who echoes a more traditional Reformed and catholic view on these issues. Vos asks this question: "*Does not the creation of the universe detract from the immutability of God?*"[90] He answers:

88. Frame, *Systematic Theology*, 376–77; emphasis original. Technically speaking, divine relenting (or repenting) is termed anthropopathic not anthropomorphic.

89. Weinandy, *Does God Change?*, 169. The citation for the Donceel reference is Joseph Donceel, "Second Thoughts on the Nature of God," *Thought*, 46 (1971), p. 351. In the footnote to this reference, Weinandy says, "[Donceel] seems to opt for a mitigated form of Process Theology. 'According to this modified form of theism God is Pure Act, yet he contains potency. He is Being itself, yet he becomes; he is immutable, although he changes. He is eternal, but in time; he is omniscient, but he finds out from man what man freely decides,' (p. 365)." This sounds dangerously similar to Frame's claim.

90. Vos, *Reformed Dogmatics*, 1:177.

No, when Scripture appears to speak as if there is a succession and change in God Himself, it is expressing itself in a human way. For example, in Psalm 90, where the absolute eternity of God is taught so clearly, it is however also said, "Before the mountains were born and You had brought forth the earth and the world, yes, from everlasting to everlasting You are God." (v. 2). The word "before" appears to introduce time into eternity, but that is because of the weakness of human language.[91]

... time and differences of time are products of creation, not the forms in which the creating God Himself moves.[92]

Mascall's words echo Vos's.

It is, of course, true that, as we view him, God appears to be subject to change; because the universe that he has created is a changing universe, God's action upon it when viewed from within it appears to be a changing action. Nevertheless, the change that is observed is not a change in God but in his creation . . ."[93]

In 2012, Oliphint said, "I happen to believe as well that the other *principium* of the Reformation—the doctrine of God—was itself not sufficiently re-tooled in light of Reformed theology . . ."[94] In *God with Us*, published in 2012, Oliphint says, "In chapter 2, I will begin to outline a way of thinking about God's voluntary condescension. This chapter will begin to introduce a relatively new approach to a discussion of God's character."[95] This assumes previous approaches were either wrong or, at least, need some sort of modification. In 2014, Oliphint said, "[M]uch of systematic theology that is done, especially in theology proper, needs a complete revision and rewrite."[96] This statement was made in the context of Oliphint advocating that we be "fearlessly anthropomorphic" in our formulations of the doctrine of God.[97] "Oliphint has expressed that several 'brilliant' theologians, viz., Augustine,

91. Vos, *Reformed Dogmatics*, 1:177–78.

92. Vos, *Reformed Dogmatics*, 1:178.

93. Mascall, *He Who Is*, 100.

94. K. Scott Oliphint, "Aquinas: A Shaky Foundation." Available at https://www.thegospelcoalition.org/article/aquinas-a-shaky-foundation/. Accessed 4 November 2017.

95. Oliphint, *God with Us*, 43.

96. K. Scott Oliphint, "Theological Principles from Van Til's Common Grace and the Gospel." Lecture delivered at the 2014 Reformed Forum Theology Conference, Gray's Lake, IL, October 2014. http://reformedforum.org/rf14_08/. Accessed 30 March 2015.

97. Ironically, Oliphint's proposals are less than "fearlessly anthropomorphic"; they appear, rather, to be fearlessly non-anthropomorphic. I owe this statement to Glen Clary.

Aquinas, Stephen Charnock, Paul Helm, and Herman Bavinck failed to be 'fearlessly anthropomorphic' . . ."[98] In *The Majesty of Mystery* (2016), after identifying various Old Testament theophanies, Oliphint says:

> There is an abundance of literature that deals with these issues, much of which can be pursued with great profit. However, even some of the best theologians in the history of the church misstep when pressed with questions like the ones above [e.g., How can God walk in the garden and appear to Abraham if he is spirit with no body?]. Unfortunately, examples are almost too numerous to list.[99]

Let the reader ponder the implications of Oliphint's claim. Theologians of the Christian tradition who misstep by not being fearlessly anthropomorphic are "almost too numerous to list." In other words, the Christian tradition is substantially wrong on this issue.

After offering Augustine, Charnock, and Bavinck as examples, Oliphint says:

> As admirable as these motives are, however, it is not in keeping with biblical language and emphases to think, speak, or write in such ways as these great theologians have done. We have to find a better way to interpret biblical passages dealing with God and His relations to the world.[100]

Again, let the reader ponder these words. Admirable motives aside, these great theologians are in error on a crucial element of the doctrine of God.

It should be obvious by now that Oliphint does not agree with the traditional, classical Christian, and Reformed account of many of the

98. Brandon F. Smith and James M. Renihan, "Historical Theology Survey of the Doctrine of Divine Impassibility: The Modern Era," in *Confessing the Impassible God*, 273. Smith and Renihan are quoting from Oliphint's 2014 lecture, "Theological Principles." For a published version of that section of the lecture see Cornelius Van Til, *Common Grace and the Gospel*, Second Edition, ed. K. Scott Oliphint (Phillipsburg, NJ: P&R Publishing, 2015), x–xxv. What might be of interest to some readers is the fact that in this Foreword by Oliphint, he recommends his *God with Us* "[f]or an extended, book-length answer to this question" (*Common Grace and the Gospel*, xvii, n. 14). "This question" refers to "how one can affirm, as Van Til does, *both* that 'God's attitude has changed with respect to mankind' *and* that 'God in himself is changeless'" (*Common Grace and the Gospel*, xvii). Oliphint also recommends *God with Us* in his *Covenantal Apologetics: Principles & Practice in Defense of Our Faith* (Phillipsburg, NJ: P&R Publishing, 2013), 58, n. 2, 62, n. 7, 82, n. 26, 183, n. 17, and 234, n. 7. The basic thesis of *God with Us* is repeated on page 190 of Oliphint's *Covenantal Apologetics*.

99. Oliphint, *The Majesty of Mystery*, 91.

100. Oliphint, *The Majesty of Mystery*, 93–94.

metaphorical assertions of Scripture pertaining to God.[101] Indeed, it appears that he views his book *The Majesty of Mystery* as articulating "a better way to interpret biblical passages dealing with God and His relations to the world." What does Oliphint view as going wrong in the Christian theological tradition in terms of accounting for the metaphorical assertions of Scripture pertaining to God's actions toward creation? He tells us, at least in part, in the following words. He says, "Thomas Aquinas, whose doctrine of God can, in places, be consistent with that which was emphasized at the time of the Reformation, nevertheless stumbled as his mentor, Augustine, had done."[102] The following words occur as a footnote to this statement.

> My own conviction is that, since Aquinas, too many have adopt-
> ed his ideas and language, especially with respect to his doctrine
> of God, and thus have had no clear and cogent way to affirm
> much, if not most, of what Scripture says about God and his
> dealings with, and activity in, creation.[103]

So, in Oliphint's view, the problem with the traditional way to account for God's *ad extra* works goes all the way back to Augustine but seems to fall more at the feet of Aquinas and the "too many [who] have adopted his ideas and language, especially with respect to his doctrine of God . . ."

We must admit that there are many difficult issues presented to us by the language of Scripture when it comes to assertions about God. Our interest in the language of Scripture, however, is not the mere words used, but the divine intent. The older way of accounting for the metaphorical assertions

---

101. A further example of this can be found in *God with Us*, 220, where Oliphint says, "In condescending to interact with his people, the Lord did relent from what he would otherwise have done. This is in no way an improper or metaphorical way of speaking" and in *God with Us*, 227–28, where he says, "The point of the passage [i.e., Gen. 22:12], however, is not that God knows the end from the beginning in any and every situation or in Abraham's life, *true as that is*. The point of the passage is that God's covenant with his people, and with Abraham as the father of his people, is one that really and truly, *not simply metaphorically* [emphasis added], involves God in the process. It is a commitment in which he has come down, covenantally 'hiding' those essential properties that remain his, in order to bind himself to us and to our lives in such a way that his interaction with us involves a real, ongoing, empathetic relationship. He really does identify with us, and he moves with us in history, 'learning' and listening, in order to maintain and manage the covenant relationship that he has sovereignly and unilaterally established, the details of which he has eternally and immutably decreed." Again, ironically, Oliphint's proposals are less than "fearlessly anthropomorphic."

102. Van Til, *Common Grace and the Gospel*, xiv.

103. Van Til, *Common Grace and the Gospel*, xiv, n. 8.

of Scripture pertaining to God is both better and keeps one in the bounds of Christian orthodoxy.[104]

QUESTIONS TO PONDER

An important question comes to mind in light of the discussion above. Assuming that God does, in fact, have two existences, what gets revealed to creatures? If God's atemporal mode of existence is not his temporal or historical mode of existence, if his temporal or historical mode of existence is not eternal, then would it not follow that, since his temporal mode is his revelational mode, the eternal mode of existence, or the eternal God as such, is not revealed to us? If both modes are revealed, why the need for a second, historical mode? If the answer is because the atemporal mode cannot be revealed to creatures for ontological reasons, does not this point surrender an aspect of the doctrine of God to something dangerously close to process theism? If it does (and it seems inescapable that it does), has any reputable theologian of the Reformed theological tradition ever surrendered such ground and remained within the bounds of Reformed confessional orthodoxy? It is difficult to know the answer to the last question, though one may surmise. It is time for those who claim the confession and posit two modes of existence in God to sit down, think long and hard about the entailments of such a proposal, and ask and answer the kinds of questions mentioned above.

In *God with Us*, Oliphint says this, explaining what he means when he asserts that God has condescended:

> We mean that God freely determined to take on attributes, characteristics, and properties that he did not have, and would not have, without creation. In his taking these characteristics, we understand as well that whatever characteristics or attributes he takes on, they cannot be of the essence of who he is, nor can they be necessary to his essential identity as God. In other words, given that whatever properties he takes on as a result of his free knowledge and will, he did not *have* to take them on; he could have chosen not to create or decree anything. Thus, his condescension means that he is *adding* properties and characteristics, not to his essential being, as the triune God (since that would mean that God was essentially mutable), but surely to himself (more on this later).[105]

---

104. Accounting for the older way is beyond the scope of this book.

105. Oliphint, *God with Us*, 110. For objections to this aspect of Oliphint's argument

By the words "more on this later," it is assumed that Oliphint is referring to his importing of Christological/incarnational categories back into the Old Testament. Whether that is the case or not, it is no secret that Oliphint proposes that Christology is to guide theology proper.[106] Christology, for Oliphint, is the lens through which God's *ad extra* works are to be understood. He says, ". . . christology organizes our understanding of God's relationality."[107] It is beyond the scope of the present critique to interact with this aspect of Oliphint's thesis. It may well be the driving, methodological force behind all that he says regarding covenantal properties.[108] This critique is limited

---

see Duby, *Divine Simplicity*, where he says, "An assessment of Oliphint's location of the freedom of the decree in God's 'covenantal condescnesion' is beyond this study. It may be said, however, that it is based on a problematic supposition that God can assume (in an anticipatory relation to the incarnation) properties of a creaturely nature without having yet assumed such a nature in the incarnation . . ." (198, n. 66). Dolezal in "Objections to K. Scott Oliphint's Covenantal Properties Thesis" mentions and discusses three concerns: "First, if the human properties of the incarnate Son are not divine attributes, then neither are the 'covenantal properties' that Oliphint proposes for God. After all, what is assumed in the Son's incarnation is wholly creature and is in no way to be regarded as divine. . . . Second, it is difficult to see how Oliphint's incarnational model does not entail that the Father and Spirit each subsist as one person in two ontologically distinct ways, just as the Son does by his subsistence in two natures. . . . Third, and perhaps even more perplexing, is the implication Oliphint's incarnational model has for the Son. If he, with the Father and Spirit, experiences the union of divine and covenantal, then he already subsists in this divine/creature union prior to his incarnation. . . ." Rennie, "Appendix I," in *Confessing the Impassible God*, 404–05, also provides critique. For example, he says: "Oliphint maintains that this notion of covenantal properties is 'affirmed in christology.' . . . In short, God has taken on created properties from the foundation of the world in the same way that the Son of God took on created human properties in the incarnation. 'What is true of the incarnation is true also of other 'incarnations' of God in Scripture' (192). . . . Such a proposal raises several unhappy consequences. For instance, are we to apply the concept to each person of the Trinity, or just the Son? . . . On the one hand, if it is consistently applied to each, we must conclude one of two things. Either we are to conceive of these properties accidentally, and therefore reject divine simplicity, or they are to be conceived of substantially. Oliphint appears to prefer the latter, arguing that in the incarnation, the Son of God did not merely take on accidental properties, but rather assumed a substantial union of two natures in one person ([*God with Us*,] 152–54). If this is so, then we are led to the unfortunate conclusion that all three persons have had two substantial natures, one created, and one divine, from the foundation of the world. It would seem difficult, therefore, to escape the conclusion that all three persons, to a greater or lesser extent, have been incarnate at one point or another. . . ." See also the Appendix in this book by Cameron G. Porter.

106. See Oliphint, *God with Us*, 136 and 183.

107. Oliphint, *God with Us*, 116.

108. See Camden Bucey, "Addressing the Essential-Covenantal Model of Theology Proper." Available at https://reformedforum.org/addressing-the-essential-covenantal-model-of-theology-proper/. Accessed 5 June 2019. Bucey addresses this aspect of Oliphint's proposal under the heading "The Addition of Christology."

to the aspects of his thesis and its entailments, and does not critique its methodological basis. Suffice it to say, Oliphint's method is not a safe guide. It seems to be a category error. It puts a redemptive category before a more basic revelational category and, if not checked, runs the risk of reading the *oikonomia* back into the *theologia*. It makes the incarnation of our Lord the climax of lesser "incarnations"[109] which precede it. God, however, is not ever-incarnating himself in redemptive history. Frame seems to attempt the same thing as Oliphint in terms of using the incarnation as an interpretive paradigm for Old Testament theophanies. Recall the words of McGraw cited above: "Much more could be said about Frame's *Systematic Theology* that illustrates where he suffers from a paucity of historical theology, such as . . . importing the two natures of Christ into pre-incarnate theophanies."

The condescension of God advocated by Oliphint comes about due to his "free knowledge and will." It is a willed mode of assumed "attributes, characteristics, and properties that he did not have, and would not have, without creation." The new features of the condescended God, though decreed, are not "of the essence of who he is, nor can they be necessary to his essential identity as God." These assumed features of God are added "to himself" but "not to his essential being." They appear to be accidental divine properties. If these features are not added "to his essential being," if they are not infinite, eternal, immutable, and impassible, if they were willed by God, are they God or not God? There is only two options; either they are God or part of the world. And if it is via these assumed covenantal properties that the condescended God reveals himself to creatures, what do creatures come into contact with through this kind of revelation or mode of condescension? Is it the eternal God, or some sort of finite, temporal, mutable, passible, willed version of God?

Oliphint is in print saying he has introduced us to "a relatively new approach to a discussion of God's character."[110] How relatively new is it? Are there others in the Reformed theological tradition who have posited covenantal condescension, the type that advocates God willing himself to take on new attributes that "he did not have, and would not have, without creation"?[111] Is Oliphint's proposal his attempt to re-tool the doctrine of God "in light of Reformed theology . . ."?[112] Recall these words of Oliphint: "[M]uch of systematic theology that is done, especially in theology proper,

109. Oliphint, *God with Us*, 76.
110. Oliphint, *God with Us*, 43.
111. Oliphint, *God with Us*, 110.
112. Oliphint, "Aquinas: A Shaky Foundation."

needs a complete revision and rewrite."[113] If this is the beginning of such a rewrite, it is fair to ask what the end will look like.

It is time for those who claim the confession and posit covenantal properties as something new in or added to God to sit down, think long and hard about the entailments of such a proposal, and ask and answer the kinds of questions mentioned above.

It is very important to distinguish between modes of existence and modes of revelation. God, as God, "has" only one mode of existence; his simple, infinite, eternal, immutable, impassible, trinitarian mode, or we might simply say the divine mode of existence. But the infinite God has mysteriously revealed himself through a multitude of finite revelational modalities. These modalities tell us something true about the divine, the infinite One, the eternal One, the immutable One, the impassible One. And the author of this kind of revelation just is God, eternal, immortal, the only wise One, Father, Son, and Holy Spirit.

Recall the words of the confession:

> In the beginning it pleased God the Father, Son, and Holy Spirit, for the manifestation of the glory of His eternal power, wisdom, and goodness, to create or make the world, and all things therein, whether visible of invisible, in the space of six days, and all very good. (2LCF 4.1)

There is no hint in the confession of some sort of change in God, necessary or willed, in order for God to create and/or manifest himself to creatures. There is no change in God given creation or not. God is not simple, infinite, eternal, immutable, and impassible in himself then, in addition, becomes composed, finite, temporal, mutable, and passible in order to create and/or manifest himself to us. The revealed mystery of it all is that the simple, infinite, eternal, immutable, and impassible God has manifested himself to creatures without any change in him. This surely is grounds for humility toward and praise of him.

CONCLUSION

This chapter has investigated a small sliver of contemporary theology. Such interaction is necessary when important issues are at stake. The critique offered above was given to challenge views which stray from important Reformed-confessional and historical, or classical Christian, boundaries. Predicating change in God by virtue of creation and relation to creatures

---

113. Oliphint, "Theological Principles from Van Til's Common Grace and the Gospel."

(or in any sense) is a move in a dangerous, even toxic, direction. It has consequences which end up compromising many long-held and clearly-argued elements of the doctrine of God. For those subscribing the WCF or its related confessions, it wreaks havoc upon the system of doctrine contained therein. The views critiqued above are idiosyncratic and contradict the confession. When novelties arise they must be questioned and scrutinized. Surely this ought to be the case with reference to the doctrine of God, the *principium essendi* of Reformed Orthodoxy. We must not cater to the age in which we live. If that were done by all who went before us, we would be in big trouble. Though we may have to stand contrary to some who have been our teachers on various matters, stand we must. If what some are advocating in our day as in step with confessional Reformed thought is not, in fact, in step with what is clearly and emphatically stated in and meant by the confessional documents, what else can confessional people do but stand against such teaching? It is the only honest thing to do. It is fully realized that some will balk at such a statement when it comes to the issues discussed above. Some think the finer, more technical elements of the doctrine of God are tertiary issues. Those subscribing the confession ought to beg to differ. Theology, as John Webster says, involves God and all things in relation to God. Get God wrong and one will get wrong various aspects of all things in relation to God. The stakes are very high, indeed.[114]

May this discussion cause those who posit some sort of change in God in order for God to be God with us to reconsider their views. What is lost by such a formulation is a price too high to pay. One loses divine simplicity, pure actuality, infinity, eternity, immutability, and impassibility. And in losing these doctrines, one forfeits the biblical teaching, the classical Christian doctrine of God, and the Reformed confession.

114. Having said that, we ought to remember that our better intuitions are often more orthodox than our idiosyncratic arguments and the Lord is way more merciful than we realize. The last clause is basically a re-word of what I once heard a trusted friend say. He is right.

6

Confessing Trinitarian Creation

The Doctrine of Appropriations in John Owen's "Peculiar Works of the Holy Spirit in the First or Old Creation"

"GOD MINUS THE WORLD is still God the Holy Trinity," says Fred Sanders.[1] The following words are a fitting addition to Sanders's: "God plus the world is still God the Holy Trinity." In other words, given creation or not, God is still God the Holy Trinity. Creation does not change God, nor does God change God *in order to* create or relate to creation. No work of God changes God in any sense whatsoever. God's works reveal him. God is neither enhanced by what comes into being nor self-enhanced in order to cause things to come into being. Webster says, "[N]o enhancement of God is achieved by the world's existence."[2] Creatures are brought into contingent being without any change in the supreme being, who is God, the non-contingent cause of all contingent being. Creation is actuated, that is, caused, or effected. God the Trinity—Father, Son, and Holy Spirit—caused that which has come into being to come into being without any change of being in divine being. The "change" (i.e., creatures) goes forth from God's being eternally and is reflective of that being, however. If change occurs in God due to creation or

---

1. Fred Sanders, *The Deep Things of God: how the Trinity changes everything* (Wheaton, IL: Crossway, 2010), 63.

2. Webster, *God without Measure*, 1:91.

anything else, God would not be immutable, for example, in any meaningful sense. Confessing trinitarian creation requires that God remains God in the same sense God is God without creation. God *just is*, full stop. He is God, whether creation or not creation, and the God who *just is* is the three persons, or subsistences, we call the blessed Trinity. If one posits change in God due to creation or anything else, one denies divine simplicity, infinity, eternity, immutability and impassibility, no matter how loudly he attempts to affirm either or both. For example, God is either immutable or mutable. God is either simple or compounded. There is no *tertium quid* (i.e., a third something) option in God. Once any one of the divine perfections is compromised, all other divine perfections go with it. These basic, foundational elements of our confessed theology proper are important to remember while discussing creation.

This chapter focuses on two aspects of confession 4.1. The first is an explicit assertion concerning trinitarian creation and the second is an implicit assertion to the same end. The explicit assertion is straightforward and will be discussed in the next section. The implicit assertion is a bit veiled to the modern reader, however. Acquainting ourselves with the historical discussion concerning the Trinity and creation prior to the formulation of the confession helps us understand what is meant by "it pleased God the Father, Son, and Holy Spirit, for the manifestation of the glory of His eternal *power, wisdom*, and *goodness* . . ." (emphases added). The triad of "power, wisdom, and goodness" in the context of confessing creation in relation to the Trinity has a history which pre-dates the confession and sheds light on its meaning in it. The first concern in this chapter, however, is the explicit assertion concerning trinitarian creation at 4.1. To that we will now turn our attention.

THE EXPLICIT ASSERTION OF TRINITARIAN CREATION IN THE CONFESSION

The confession of trinitarian creation is explicit in these words: ". . . it pleased God the *Father, Son, and Holy Spirit* . . . to create . . . the world . . ." (emphases added). It is of interest to point out that this is not the first time trinitarian creation is explicitly confessed by a Reformation-era symbol. The Confession of the Evangelical Church in Germany of 1614 in its third article says this:

> We believe and confess that the one true God, the Father, Son, and Holy Spirit, created heaven and earth and all things out of nothing. For it is written: "In the beginning God created heaven

and earth" (Gen. 1:1). "All things were made through the Word" (that is, through the Son of God) (John 1:3; Col. 1:16; Heb. 1:2). "The heavens were made by the Word of the Lord and all His host by the breath of His mouth" (Ps. 33:6).[3]

Not only is explicit trinitarian creation clear, but the cited Scripture texts are very typical in such discussions.

The Scripture texts cited in 2LCF to support the explicit trinitarian formulation on creation are as follows:

> He was in the beginning with God. All things were made through Him, and without Him nothing was made that was made (John 1:2–3)

> has in these last days spoken to us by *His* Son, whom He has appointed heir of all things, through whom also He made the worlds (Heb. 1:2)

> By His Spirit He adorned the heavens; His hand pierced the fleeing serpent (Job 26:13)

> For since the creation of the world His invisible *attributes* are clearly seen, being understood by the things that are made, *even* His eternal power and Godhead, so that they are without excuse (Rom. 1:20)

> For by Him all things were created that are in heaven and that are on earth, visible and invisible, whether thrones or dominions or principalities or powers. All things were created through Him and for Him (Col. 1:16)

> Then God saw everything that He had made, and indeed *it was* very good. So the evening and the morning were the sixth day. (Gen. 1:31)

These texts (and others) were utilized for many centuries to ground this doctrine in Holy Scripture.[4] Creation is a work of God, a work of Father, Son, and Holy Spirit as such. It is an undivided work of the Trinity. As Webster asserts, "In the economy the Trinity acts indivisibly, and the works of the Trinity are to be attributed 'absolutely' to the one divine essence."[5]

---

3. Dennison, *Reformed Confessions*, 4:57.

4. See Paul M. Blowers, *Drama of the Divine Economy: Creator and creation in Early Christian Theology and Piety* (Oxford, UK: Oxford University Press, 2012).

5. Webster, *God without Measure*, 1:94.

"There was no intra-trinitarian counsel where divine persons parceled out various aspects of the divine creative activity."[6] In other words, though the Bible attributes the work of creation to each of the divine persons, this does not entail it was divided up or distributed among a divine community. We must not think of the work of creation as one-third effected by the Father, one-third effected by the Son, and one-third effected by the Holy Spirit. Nor ought we to think of it as one-half effected by the Son and one-half effected by the Spirit, as if the Father alone appointed the Son and Spirit as subordinate agents to carry-out his work. As Gill says with reference to the Son, creation came about "not by him as an instrument, but as co-efficient cause."[7] This applies to the Holy Spirit just the same. The *ad extra* works of the Trinity are undivided works. The Latin is *opera Trinitatis ad extra sunt indivisa* (i.e., The external works of the Trinity are undivided.). Muller explains this doctrine as follows:

> . . . since the Godhead is one in essence, one in knowledge, and one in will, it would be impossible in any work *ad extra* . . . for one of the divine persons to will and to do one thing and another of the divine persons to will and do another.[8]

This is crucial to uphold throughout our accounting for the divine economy, lest we lose the Trinity doctrine. As Webster says, "divine works in respect of creatures may not be assigned severally to Father, Son and Holy Spirit as to quasi-independent agents."[9] When God acts, it is the triune God who acts. We must admit, however, that though these acts are undivided, they are revealed to us after a trinitarian theological grammar for which we must account in order to protect the unity of essence (unity of essence is confessed in 2.1) in the undivided work. How ought this to be accomplished?

Before answering this question, it may be helpful to consider some biblical texts which illustrate that for which we need to account.

> By the word of the LORD the heavens were made, And all the host of them by the breath of His mouth. (Psalm 33:6)

> 'You are worthy, O Lord, To receive glory and honor and power; For You created all things, And by Your will they exist and were created.' (Rev. 4:11)

---

6. In the process of writing, at some point I inserted this sentence into my notes without attribution. I am not sure of its source.

7. Gill, *A Body of Doctrinal and Practical Divinity*, 260.

8. Muller, *Dictionary*, 246.

9. Webster, *God without Measure*, 1:94.

yet for us *there is* one God, the Father, of whom *are* all things, and we for Him; and one Lord Jesus Christ, through whom *are* all things, and through whom we *live*. (1 Cor. 8:6)

In the beginning was the Word, and the Word was with God, and the Word was God. 2 He was in the beginning with God. 3 All things were made through Him, and without Him nothing was made that was made. (John 1:1–3)

For by Him [i.e., the Son of the Father's love] all things were created that are in heaven and that are on earth, visible and invisible, whether thrones or dominions or principalities or powers. All things were created through Him and for Him. (Col. 1:16)

And the Spirit of God was hovering over the face of the waters. (Gen 1:2)

By His Spirit He adorned the heavens (Job 26:13)

O Lord, how manifold are Your works! In wisdom You have made them all. The earth is full of Your possessions (Psalm 104:24)

You send forth Your Spirit, they are created (Psalm 104:30)

These texts (and others) are those for which we must account. Are there three Creators or, as noted above, are there three who create? All the orthodox confess one Creator, God. But how has Christian orthodoxy accounted for the scriptural assertions which attribute creation to the Father, creation to the Son, and creation to the Holy Spirit, while maintaining the unity of essence and the undivided acts of the Trinity in the work of creation? To this we now give attention.

THE IMPLICIT ASSERTION OF TRINITARIAN CREATION IN THE CONFESSION

There is an implicit assertion of trinitarian creation at confession 4.1 in the following words: "for the manifestation of the glory of His eternal *power, wisdom, and goodness*" (emphases added). Why is this the case and how can it be proven? The confession reads: "it pleased God the Father, Son, and Holy Spirit, for the manifestation of the glory of His [i.e., the triune God's] eternal power, wisdom, and goodness, to create . . ." The triad, "power, wisdom, and goodness," has a unique development in the history of theology which will be discussed below. For now, it is important to affirm that "power, wisdom, and goodness" are natural, or essential, attributes of the divine essence and, therefore, common to the Father, Son, and Holy Spirit. All three of the terms in this triad are eternal perfections of the triune God. All three may be predicated properly of Father, Son, and Holy Spirit. No one person of the Godhead is anything the other persons are not in terms of the divine essence. No one person of the Godhead is more of the divine essence than the others. If that were not the case, the person or persons with less of the divine essence would not be divine, or God, in the proper sense. That person or those persons would be god-light. Eternal power, wisdom, and goodness ought to and must be predicated properly of the Father, the Son, and the Holy Spirit lest we lose the Trinity.

In the process of research for this book, one of the things that was necessary was to read theologians of the seventeenth century. It was found that the triad "power, wisdom, and goodness" occurs in the extant literature of the day discussing creation.[10] This tells us it was common theological grammar while discussing the doctrine of creation.[11] But was this triad first used in the seventeenth century while discussing creation? The answer is a resounding no, and there is ample evidence which substantiates this claim.

Triads, God, the Trinity, and Creation

In the history of the church, speaking of God utilizing triads goes back to at least Augustine.[12] The triad found at confession 4.1, however, came to

10. E.g., James Ussher, *A Body of Divinity: Being the Sum and Substance of the Christian Religion* (1648; reprint, Birmingham, AL: Solid Ground Christian Books, 2007), 83; Wollebius, "Compendium Theologiae Christianae," 50, 54, 56; Ames, *The Marrow of Theology*, I.viii.57 (105).

11. The triad is used in the context of the creation of man in The Formula Consensus Helvetica of 1675, but the three terms are predicated of God naturally or essentially. "As all his works were known unto God from eternity (Acts 15:18), so in time, according to his infinite power, wisdom, and goodness, he made man . . ." Dennison, *Reformed Confessions*, 4:522. About 100 years prior, The Confession of La Rochelle (1571) confessed: "We believe that God, in three cooperating persons, has—by His power, His wisdom, and His incomprehensible goodness—created all things . . ." Dennison, *Reformed Confessions*, 3:309.

12. The phenomenon of triadic predication with reference to God finds its roots in Holy Scripture itself. See Ryan M. McGraw, *Knowing the Trinity: Practical Thoughts for Daily Life* (Lancaster, PA: Alliance of Confessing Evangelicals, 2017), 115–37. McGraw provides an appendix with over 20 pages of "Triadic Passages in Scripture."

be utilized while discussing trinitarian creation in a unique manner in the medieval period. Emery says:

> It was Abelard who made this triad famous, but it appears to have been Hugh of St. Victor . . . [to whom] we owe the link-ing of the triad, *power, wisdom,* and *goodness* to the Father, Son, and Holy Spirit. Hugh of St. Victor knew this triad of divine attributes from his patristic sources . . . [but he] made a light and sparing use of it. When Peter Abelard took this triadic formula over from Hugh, it took on a primary role, and this primary role was something out of the ordinary.
>
> . . . One of the main features of Abelard's thesis consisted in disclosing the three divine persons on the basis of power, wis-dom, and benevolence . . . the Father 'is called Father because of the unique power of his majesty'; the Son is called Son 'because one can see authentic wisdom in him'; and the Holy Spirit is so called 'according to the grace of his goodness.'[13]

According to Emery, Abelard identified a potential problem with such a formulation.

> Abelard could see perfectly well for himself that the problem raised by this analysis is how to use these attributes to distin-guish the persons, given that one acknowledges that they also designate that which is divine as such, or that power, wisdom, and goodness are common to the three persons.[14]

So what did he do? As with Turretin later, he distinguished. Listen to Emery again:

> So, within the statements we make about the Triune God, one must distinguish those which touch on the common identity (the power shared by the three persons), and those which deal with the distinct property of a person (where we are attributing wisdom and benevolence to Father, Son, and Holy Spirit). The words 'power, wisdom, goodness' can thus contain two differ-ent meanings, dependent on the context: the one personal, the other substantial, that is, shared by all three persons.[15]

---

13. Giles Emery, *The Trinitarian Theology of St. Thomas Aquinas* (Oxford; New York: Oxford University Press, 2007), 313–14.

14. Emery, *The Trinitarian Theology of St. Thomas,* 314–15.

15. Emery, *The Trinitarian Theology of St. Thomas,* 315.

Power, wisdom, and goodness can refer to the personal properties of distinct divine persons revealed to us in the economy without denying substantial unity.

Why was this background material presented? Simply to show that, in the articulation of trinitarian creation, theologians began to utilize this triad in their discussions. (In fact, a friend of mine emailed me a few years ago, saying something to this effect, "This triad is all over the late medieval discussions of the Trinity and creation.") So when it makes its way into the confession at 4.1, it is not appearing *de novo*.

The Doctrine of Appropriations and the Confession

The phenomenon of attributing distinct external works to individual persons of the Trinity has a technical name. It is called the doctrine of appropriations. Here is what it asserts: "[The] attribution of an essential reality, of a divine action, or of a created effect (common to the three divine persons) to one person in a special way."[16] The doctrine of appropriations claims that sometimes the Bible attributes the common, external, divine work of creation to a particular divine person. We saw this in the biblical texts cited above; for example, "By His Spirit He adorned the heavens" (Job 26:13). The question then becomes this: How do we account for this in light of the fact that the external works of the Trinity are undivided? If the external works of the Trinity are undivided, how do we account for the biblical pattern of attributing peculiar divine works to particular divine persons?

Prior to answering that very important question, it is of interest to note The Hungarian *Confessio Catholica* (1562). It not only mentions undivided *ad extra* operations but it also discusses concepts such as absolute and relative predication and essential and personal predication (i.e., attribution). Here is its article entitled "The Works of the Trinity."

> The works of the Trinity are either *ad extra* or common to the whole Trinity and the three persons; as the Trinity has one essence, authority, power, will, and undivided action. So also are the works of the Trinity *ad extra* undivided, equally fitting to each person with regard to the Trinity, as creation, salvation, redemption, election, reconciliation (as is stated in Isa. 26, 44, 44 [*sic*]; 2 Cor.5). Others are inward (*ad intra*) or peculiar (*singularia*), which appertain only to the person individually and

16. Emery, *Trinity*, 199. See the discussion in Richard A. Muller, *Post-Reformation Reformed Dogmatics: The Rise and Development of Reformed Orthodoxy, ca. 1520 to ca. 1725, Volume Four, The Triunity of God* (Grand Rapids: Baker Academic, 2003), 267–74.

distinctly. And these, for the purpose of instruction, we divide
into two: the substantial and the official.[17]

Here is the same confession on "Concerning the Names and Titles of God."

> Some things about God we say essentially (*essentialiter*) and
> absolutely. That is everything that applies to the three per-
> sons and signifies the one essence is predicated substantially
> (*substantialiter*) and absolutely, as God, Lord, Spirit, to create,
> to save, substance (*substantiam*), omnipresence (Tertullian,
> Cyprian, Irenaeus, Hesychius). For just as with the Greeks, the
> substance is sometimes used for the whole essential being and
> sometimes for one definite person. Thus nature, Lord, and God
> are often made use of relatively for the person and absolutely
> for the *ousia*. But some things relatively are predicated of God
> as Father, Son, Mediator, sacrificial priest, High Priest, propi-
> tiator, Holy Spirit; in short, all those things which are suited
> to the person distinctly, are predicated relatively according to
> office and property.[18]

These citations of The Hungarian *Confessio Catholica* prove that as of
1562 the doctrines of undivided works (or inseparable operations) and appropriations (to be further discussed below) were contained in a Reformation-era symbol. Around the same time-frame as The Hungarian *Confessio*,
The Confession of Tarcal (1562) and Torda (1563) confessed inseparable
operations under the title "Article III. The Workings of the Holy Trinity Are
Inseparable One from Another."

> We so ascribe the several properties to the three persons, Father,
> Son, and Holy Spirit, that as concerns providence, creation, the
> government of the world and all things pertaining to the divine
> essence, we separate neither the Son nor the Holy Spirit from
> the Father.[19]

If the assessment of the seventeenth-century confessions under consideration given above is correct, this proves that confessing both inseparable
operations and appropriations is not novel to them; they imported the substance of previous discussions into their formulations.

The contention is that the confession reflects the doctrine of appropriations when it asserts ". . . it pleased God the Father, Son, and Holy
Spirit, for the manifestation of the glory of His eternal power, wisdom, and

---

17. Dennison, *Reformed Confessions*, 2:461–62.

18. Dennison, *Reformed Confessions*, 2:462.

19. Dennison, *Reformed Confessions*, 2:655.

goodness, to create or make the world . . ." Though "power, wisdom, and goodness" could refer to substantial unity, the context in which this triad occurs in the confession points in another direction. The context is creation by "God the Father, Son, and Holy Spirit." The triad reflects the doctrine of appropriations, illustrating that by creation the divine power of the Father, the divine wisdom of the Son, and the divine goodness of the Holy Spirit are manifested to us in distinct ways, while upholding substantial unity.

John Owen on Appropriation, Creation, the Trinity, and the Holy Spirit

John Owen will now be utilized as an example of a seventeenth-century Reformed theologian who utilizes the doctrine of appropriations in the context of discussing creation. His discussion concentrates on the work of the Holy Spirit in the old creation, but it illustrates what has been discussed. It is an example of the very method advocated above.

In Owen's *A Discourse Concerning the Holy Spirit*, book 1, chapter 4, entitled, "Peculiar works of the Holy Spirit in the first or old creation," he prefaces his discussion with these words:

> INTENDING to treat of *the operations of the Holy Ghost*, or those which are peculiar unto him, some things must be premised concerning the operation of the *Godhead* in general . . . and they are such as are needful to guide us in many passages of the Scripture, and to direct us aright in the things in particular which now lie before us.[20]

Owen then offers two points of consideration in order to account properly for "the operation of the *Godhead*." These two premises are assumed in his subsequent discussion. He says:

> 1. That all *divine operations* are usually ascribed unto *God absolutely*.[21]
> 2. Whereas the *order of operation* among the distinct persons depends on the *order of their subsistence* in the blessed Trinity, in every great work of God, the *concluding, completing, perfecting acts* are ascribed unto the Holy Ghost.[22]

20. John Owen, *The Works of John Owen*, 23 vols., ed. William H. Goold (Edinburgh; Carlisle, PA: The Banner of Truth Trust, 1988 edition), 3:92–93.

21. Owen, *Works*, 3:93.

22. Owen, *Works*, 3:94.

In Owen's second point, he asserts "the *order of operation* among the distinct persons depends on the *order of their subsistence* in the blessed Trinity." The order of subsistence "among the distinct persons" conditions the work of God in the economy. This is an important point and will be explored below.

Before moving on, however, it is important to define the technical term "subsistence" used by Owen above. It is not hard to see that Owen believes there are three subsistences which we call the blessed Trinity. What does subsistence mean in this sense? Three subsistences clearly refers to the Father, the Son, and the Holy Spirit. On the one hand, God's "subsistence is in and of Himself" (2LCF 2.1; i.e., his aseity, or self-existence). This refers to the singular divine essence in terms of its manner of being. God is ". . . the being who exists essentially or by identity with His essence; the being who is completely self-sufficient for existence and action."[23] This self-existent, singular divine substance, however, exists, or subsists, eternally in the Father, Son, and Holy Spirit (2LCF 2.3, "three subsistences, the Father, the Word (or Son), and Holy Spirit"). Subsistences here in Owen refers to the three eternal, personal modes of existence of the one divine essence. There is substantial unity (of essence) in the three subsistences (i.e., there is one divinity, or Godhead), but the three subsistences are "distinguished by several relative properties and personal relations . . ." (2LCF 2.3). The "relative properties and personal relations" are real in God and to be distinguished from the undivided common Godhead. Ames says, "The subsistence, or manner of being [*subsistentia*] of God is his one essence so far as it has personal properties."[24] This is the doctrine of the Trinity briefly stated.

Each of Owen's points above will be analyzed in order to understand his argument. First, "all *divine operations* are usually ascribed unto *God absolutely.*" Owen's intent is clear when he says, "So it is said God made all things; and so of all other works, whether in nature or in grace."[25] For example, the work of salvation is the work of God absolutely, as is the work of creation. But Owen continues:

> And the reason hereof is, because the several persons are undivided in their operations, acting all by the same will, the same wisdom, the same power. Every person, therefore, is the author of every work of God, because each person is God, and

23. Wuellner, *Dictionary of Scholastic Philosophy*, 119.

24. Ames, *The Marrow of Theology*, 1.5.1 (88). Ames' discussion is brief but to the point. Duby's words echo Ames: "The persons do not compose God but are the one God subsisting in their peculiar relative modes. Further, the persons are not composed by essence and relation . . . but rather are the essence diversely modified and characterized in transcendental relation . . ." (Duby, *Divine Simplicity*, 233).

25. Owen, *Works*, 3:93.

the divine nature is the same undivided principle of all divine operations; and this ariseth from the unity of the persons in the same essence.[26]

Here Owen is utilizing the doctrine of the undivided works of the Trinity. If someone doubts this, these words of Owen should clear all doubt: ". . . for every divine work, and every part of every divine work, is the work of God, that is, of the whole Trinity, inseparably and undividedly."[27]

An example of inseparable and undivided operations in the work of grace and an instance of attributing the same work absolutely to God can be found comparing John 6:44, "No one can come to Me unless the Father who sent Me draws him," Matthew 11:27, "All things have been delivered to Me by My Father, and no one knows the Son except the Father. Nor does anyone know the Father except the Son, and *the one* to whom the Son wills to reveal *Him*," and John 3:3 and 5, "Jesus answered and said to him, 'Most assuredly, I say to you, unless one is born again, he cannot see the kingdom of God . . . Most assuredly, I say to you, unless one is born of water and the Spirit, he cannot enter the kingdom of God'" with 2 Corinthians 4:6, "For it is the God who commanded light to shine out of darkness, who has shone in our hearts to *give* the light of the knowledge of the glory of God in the face of Jesus Christ." The work of revealing grace is attributed to the Father (John 6:44), the Son (Matt. 11:27), and the Holy Spirit (John 3:3 and 5) peculiarly, but also absolutely to God (2 Cor. 4:6).

Then under Owen's first consideration, "That all *divine operations* are usually ascribed unto God *absolutely*," he drills a bit deeper into the doctrine of the Trinity. He says:

> But as to the manner of subsistence therein [i.e., in the same essence], there is distinction, relation, and order between and among them; and hence there is no divine work but is distinctly assigned unto each person, and eminently unto one.[28]

The point is that, though all *ad extra* divine works are common to all divine persons, some *ad extra* divine works are attributed "eminently unto one" divine person. An example of this, which we will explore below with the help of Owen, is found in Genesis 1:2, "And the Spirit of God was hovering over the face of the waters." This is an illustration of a common work of the Trinity attributed "eminently unto one" person. Maybe the words of Webster will help clear this up at this point. He says, "As Gilles Emery puts

26. Owen, *Works*, 3:93.
27. Owen, *Works*, 3:94.
28. Owen, *Works*, 3:93.

it, the 'indivisibility' axiom cannot function as 'the single lever' in giving an account of the economy. . . . Common activity is not indistinguishable activity."[29] "[P]ersonal appropriation . . . is . . . eminent or distinct attribution of a common operation to a particular person of the undivided essence."[30]

Owen continues:

> The reason, therefore, why the works of God are thus distinctly ascribed unto each person is because, in the undivided operation of the divine nature, each person doth the same work in the order of their subsistence; not one as the instrument of the other, or merely employed by the other, but as one common principle of authority, wisdom, love, and power. How come they, then, eminently to be assigned one to one person, another to another? . . . And this is done,—(1.) When any especial impression is made of the especial property of any person on any work; then is that work assigned peculiarly to that person.[31]

Owen's point is that eminent appropriation is due to trinitarian relations. In other words, the Bible attributes distinct divine acts to distinct persons of the Godhead in an attempt to reveal something of the Trinity to us. Bavinck says, "[the] immanent relations of the three persons in the divine being also manifest themselves outwardly . . . in their . . . works."[32] This is why Bavinck says later, "All things proceed from the Father, are accomplished by the Son, and are completed in the Holy Spirit."[33] Note the prepositions "from," "by," and "in." This reflects the order, or *taxis*, within the Trinity and the personal properties of each subsistence: the Father is first, or unbegotten, the Son second, or begotten, and the Holy Spirit third, or the One who proceeds from the Father and the Son (2LCF 2.3 says, "the Father is of none, neither begotten nor proceeding; the Son is eternally begotten of the Father; the Holy Spirit proceeding from the Father and the Son . . ."). It also alerts us to the fact that the appropriated works of the distinct persons are not random. As Webster says, "Appropriation is not random assignation. . . . appropriation is not individuation. And *eminent* assignation is not *exclusive* assignation."[34] In other words, attributing a work to one person does not negate the activity

---

29. Webster, *God without Measure*, 1:94. Webster is referring to Emery's book on Aquinas cited above.

30. Webster, *God without Measure*, 1:94.

31. Owen, *Works*, 3:93–94.

32. Bavinck, *RD*, 2:318.

33. Bavinck, *RD*, 2:318.

34. Webster, *God without Measure*, 1:95.

of the other persons *in the same work*, but it does highlight something of that divine person's relation to the other divine persons.

Owen's second premise to his discussion on the work of the Holy Spirit in creation is as follows:

> 2. Whereas the *order of operation* among the distinct persons depends on the *order of their subsistence* in the blessed Trinity, in every great work of God, the *concluding, completing, perfecting acts* are ascribed unto the Holy Ghost.[35]

Hopefully, given the discussion above, this is a bit clearer as to its intent. Owen here assumes his first point then states what he intends to prove from various scriptural texts; namely, that "in every great work of God, the *concluding, completing, perfecting acts* are ascribed unto the Holy Ghost." This is so because the order of subsistence conditions the manner of operation. This is why William Perkins could say, "[The Holy Spirit's] proper manner of working is to finish an action, effecting it as from the Father and the Son."[36] This kind of language is typical of Reformed Orthodoxy.[37] The *ad extra* works are accomplished by the one God, yet in every work each of the three persons works in a manner which corresponds to the order of subsistence of divine being.[38]

In the chapter we are considering in Owen, he concentrates on the works of the Holy Spirit in the old creation. Prior to his discussion of this subject he says, "Now, all the works of God may be referred unto two heads:—1. Those of *nature*; 2. Those of *grace*;—or the works of the *old* and *new* creation."[39] He treats the work of the Spirit in the old creation under two headings: his work concerning inanimate creatures in general and his work concerning man in particular.

Owen views the initial work of divine creation in Genesis 1:1 as incomplete, "for the 'earth was without form and void,' Gen. i. 2."[40] He is seeking to account for Genesis 1:1 and 2 in light of Genesis 2:1, which says,

35. Owen, *Works*, 3:94.

36. William Perkins, *A Golden Chain, or The Description of Theology* (1597; reprint, Puritan Reprints, 2010), 11.

37. For example, interacting with Herman Venema's *Institutes of Theology*, Muller says: "the Spirit also has a role in this work [i.e., of creation], specifically in 'carrying all things in creation and providence to a consummation, and in his adapting them to their several ends.' Accordingly, the 'beauty, harmony, and motion' of all things in creation are understood as the work of the Spirit" (Muller, *PRRD*, 4:271; words in single quotes are Venema's).

38. This sentence is partly dependent upon Bavinck, *RD*, 2:319.

39. Owen, *Works*, 3:95.

40. Owen, *Works*, 3:96.

"Thus the heavens and the earth, and all the host of them, were finished." He views the host of heaven as "the sun, moon, and stars, and the angels themselves,"[41] citing Deuteronomy 4:19 and 1 Kings 22:19, among other texts. The texts he cites indicate that sun, moon, stars, and angels are the host of heaven. The host of the earth "is men and beasts, with all other creatures that either grow out of it or live upon it, and are nourished by it."[42] Then he makes this important statement: "Now, the forming and perfecting of *this host* of heaven and earth is that which is assigned peculiarly to the Spirit of God; and hereby the work of creation was completed and finished."[43] He then cites Job 26:13, also referenced in the confession: "By His Spirit He adorned the heavens . . ." Commenting on the word "adorned" ("garnished" in Owen), he says, "the word signifies to 'adorn,' to make fair, to render beautiful to the eye."[44] Then he comments on this text as follows:

> Thus the heavens were garnished by the Spirit of God, when, by the creation and disposal of the aspectable [i.e., that which has the ability to be seen] host of them, he rendered them so glorious and beautiful as we behold. So the Targum, "His Spirit beautified the face of the heavens," or gave them that comely beauty and order wherein their face appeareth unto us. Hence the heavens, as adorned with the moon and stars, are said to be the "work of God's fingers," Ps. viii. 3,—that is, not only those which were powerfully made, but also curiously wrought and adorned by the Spirit of God in an especial manner intended. . . . This, then, is peculiarly assigned to the Spirit with respect to the heavens and their host : The completing, finishing work is as-cribed unto him; which we must understand by the rules before mentioned, and not exclusively to the other persons.[45]

Gill says similar things:

> . . . nor is the holy Spirit to be excluded from having a concern in the works of creation; since he . . . moved upon the face of the waters at the first creation, and brought the unformed earth into a beautiful order, and by him the heavens were garnished, and bespangled with luminaries, Gen. i. 2. Job xxvi. 13.[46]

41. Owen, *Works*, 3:95.
42. Owen, *Works*, 3:96.
43. Owen, *Works*, 3:96.
44. Owen, *Works*, 3:96.
45. Owen, *Works*, 3:96–97.
46. Gill, *A Body of Doctrinal and Practical Divinity*, 260.

Owen then sets his sight on the host of the earth, concentrating on Genesis 1:2, "The earth was without form, and void; and darkness *was* on the face of the deep. And the Spirit of God was hovering over the face of the waters." He calls the earth at this point "the whole *inferior globe*."[47] Recall that Owen views the creation of Genesis 1:1 as incomplete. As Michael Horton says, "Creation at this point was simply a good house waiting to be turned into a beautiful and well-ordered home."[48] This *"inferior globe"* includes the "material mass of earth and water."[49] Owen views the words of Genesis 1:2, "the Spirit of God was hovering," as a reference to a peculiar work of the Spirit. Then he draws this conclusion:

> This, therefore, was the work of the Holy Spirit of God in reference unto the *earth* and the *host* thereof: The whole matter being created out of which all living creatures were to be educed, and of which they were to be made, he takes upon him the cherishing and preservation of it; that as it had its subsistence by the power of the Word of God, it might be carried on towards that form, order, beauty, and perfection, that it was designed unto. To this purpose he communicated unto it a quickening and prolific virtue, inlaying it with the seeds of animal life unto all kinds of things. Hence, upon the command of God, it brought forth all sorts of creatures in abundance, according to the seeds and principles of life which were communicated unto the rude, inform chaos, by the cherishing motion of the Holy Spirit. . . . by the moving of the Spirit of God upon it, the principles of all those kinds, sorts, and forms of things, which is an inconceivable variety, make up its host and ornament, were communicated unto it. . . . And as at the first creation, so in the course of providence, the work of cherishing and nourishing the creatures is assigned in an especial manner unto the Spirit [citing Psalm 104:30]. . . . And this is the substance of what the Scripture expressly asserts concerning the work of the Spirit of God towards the inanimate part of the creation.[50]

Psalm 104:30 says, "You send forth Your Spirit, they are created; And You renew the face of the earth." Here both creation and renewal are attributed to the Spirit of God. But notice one more thing about this text. Note these words carefully: "You send forth Your Spirit." Now listen to Bavinck:

47. Owen, *Works*, 3:97.

48. Michael Horton, *Rediscovering the Holy Spirit: God's Perfecting Presence in Creation, Redemption, and Everyday Life* (Grand Rapids: Zondervan, 2017), 50.

49. Owen, *Works*, 3:97.

50. Owen, *Works*, 3:98–99.

"special properties and works are attributed to each of the three persons . . . in such a way that the order present between the persons in the ontological Trinity is revealed."[51] The *theologia* is revealed in the *oikonomia*. The mystery of the Trinity is manifested in the external works of the Trinity, sometimes explicitly indicated to us in the written word of God (e.g., Gen. 1:2). As Emery says, "In their common work of creation, the three persons act through their common nature, each person bringing his own property into play."[52] This is why Webster can say the following:

> The Holy Spirit is Lord and giver of life, creation's perfecting cause. Creation is distinctly assigned to the Spirit in that he is the divine person by whom created things are brought to the proper end. . . . By the breath of the Spirit, who is himself breathed by the Father and the Son, creatures . . . come to be alive.[53]

"You send forth Your Spirit, they are created; And You renew the face of the earth" (Psalm 104:30). The language of sending forth echoes the intra-trinitarian life of God. The Spirit is from the Father and the Son. As Horton says, commenting on Psalm 104:30, "The Spirit is not a *power emanating* but a *person sent*."[54] Though God's external works are not God (i.e., they do not constitute him nor are they emanations of him), they tell us something about the triune God who works (i.e., they manifest him). The works of God toward creatures reveal the triune God to creatures. The hovering work of the Spirit of God in Genesis 1:2 is an instance of appropriating an undivided work of the Trinity to the Holy Spirit in a peculiar way, revealing divine goodness.

CONCLUSION

Economic appropriations are grounded in intra-trinitarian personal relations. A robust theological method of trinitarian creation accounts for the *oikonomia* through the lens of the *theologia*. This is why the confession says, ". . . it pleased God the Father, Son, and Holy Spirit, for the manifestation of His eternal power, wisdom, and goodness, to create or make the world . . ." The *ad extra* divine work of creation manifests the *ad intra* divine relations. This is why we can assert that all things come from the Father, by the Son, in the Holy Spirit. This is also why the 2LCF affirms the "doctrine of the

---

51. Bavinck, *RD*, 2:318.
52. Emery, *The Trinitarian Theology of St. Thomas*, 346.
53. Webster, *God without Measure*, 1:97, 98.
54. Horton, *The Holy Spirit*, 31.

Trinity [as] the foundation of all our communion with God, and comfortable dependence on Him" (2.3). And this is why we sing:

> Praise God from whom all blessings flow;
> Praise him, all creatures here below;
> Praise him above, ye heavenly host:
> Praise Father, Son, and Holy Ghost.

These familiar words penned by our Lord's apostle are a fitting close to this discussion: "The grace of the Lord Jesus Christ, and the love of God, and the communion of the Holy Spirit *be* with you all. Amen" (2 Cor. 13:14).

7

Conclusion

We have noted the strategic placement of chapter 4 in the confession. Also noted was the importance of hermeneutics and theological method in the formulation of Christian doctrine. At 4.1, the confession clearly maintains a Creator/creature distinction. This distinction, however, does not entail a version of divine transcendence which assumes an ontological steel curtain between God and creatures. Though the ontological divide does exist, it does not keep God from us. It ever-reminds us that God is God and creatures are not.

God the Trinity is pleased to create the world. He does this "for the manifestation of the glory of His eternal power, wisdom, and goodness." God manifests himself as he is, and he is Trinity. The simple, infinite, eternal, immutable, and impassible triune God brings into existence a vast array of diverse creatures out of the fullness of his being. He brings creatures into being, sustains them, and mysteriously moves them in their ever-changing existence with no change in him. These and other truths are either explicitly or implicitly contained in confession 4.1.

The vast array of changing creatures entails no change in God. This means that even God's good gifts given to his children constitute no change in God. James 1:17 says, "Every good gift and every perfect gift is from above, and comes down from the Father of lights, with whom there is no variation or shadow of turning." It is important to understand this text in context. It comes in the context of the relation of the trials of believers to God (James 1:12–18). Verse 18 is James' example of a good and perfect gift God gives to us, referring to the new birth. In verse 17, James says good and perfect gifts come "down from the Father of lights." God as "the Father of lights" refers to God the Creator (and Sustainer) of lights (i.e., sun, moon, and stars).[1] Then James further amplifies "the Father of lights" with these important qualifying words, "with whom there is no variation or shadow of turning." Though that which God created may (and does) change, he who created does not change. In other words, God is essentially and, therefore, eternally immutable. Here God is said to be not like that which he has created. Unlike that which has come into being, he who made all things is of a different order of being. Turretin says, "The succession and flow of the parts of duration (which exist successively) necessarily involve a certain species of motion (which cannot be applied to God)."[2] James contrasts God with an aspect of his creation. As Thomas Manton said long ago, "God, and all that is in God, is unchangeable."[3] James argues from the immutability of the divine nature (v. 17) to the immutability of the divine goodness and love toward those who have been "brought . . . forth by the word of truth" (v. 18). Again, Manton says, ". . . God doth not change; there is no wrinkle upon the brow of eternity; the arm of mercy is not dried up, nor do his bowels of love waste and spend themselves."[4] God does not pass from one state of existence to another; he is who he is (Exod. 3:14; John 1:18; 4:24; 8:58; 1 John 4:8). He may communicate or reveal to us more of who he is, but that does not change who he is, though it certainly changes us. Good and perfect gifts given to us change us not God. All of God's *ad extra* works manifest him to us, but they do not deplete or change God in any sense. This is grounds for trust, worship, and service.[5]

The brief confessional formulation analyzed in this book is pregnant with doctrinal assertion and implication. It is a scriptural formulation, based on a multi-faceted theological method of accounting for a wide range

1. Notice the allusion to antecedent revelation here. The New Testament authors assume the Old Testament and its theology.

2. Turretin, *Institutes of Elenctic Theology*, 3.10.3 (1:202).

3. Thomas Manton, *An Exposition of the Epistle of James* (Grand Rapids: Associated Publishers and Authors, Inc., [n.d.]), 113.

4. Manton, *James*, 114. We might add that neither do his bowels of love increase and multiply themselves.

5. This paragraph is adapted from Richard C. Barcellos and James P. Butler, "The New Testament on the Doctrine of Divine Impassibility (I)," in *Confessing the Impassible God*, 197–98, of which I am the author.

of biblical texts, inclusive of a distinct hermeneutic. The confessional statement on creation by our triune God reflects a method that recognizes theological discussions which had been taking place for many centuries. Though
rooted in Holy Scripture, it gives evidence that the framers were not doing
theology on their own. It is not idiosyncratic. It is public theology. Though it
is a Protestant and Reformed statement, in one sense it is also a traditional,
catholic, or classical Christian statement.

In less than 50 words, confession 4.1 takes us from the inception of
creation to the ground of creation, the author of creation, the goal of cre-
ation, the essence of creation, the scope of creation, the duration of creation,
and the nature of creation. Good symbolic statements encapsulate truth in
economic fashion. Confession 4.1 certainly does that.

It is hoped that this book will assist its readers to understand better
what is contained in confession 4.1 and, more importantly, its scriptural
basis, along with the hermeneutical and theological method necessary to
account for it. Knowledge of trinitarian creation and how to account for it,
however, must not remain as a cranial exercise alone. Knowing must result
in worship, thankfulness, and service in and through the church. The desire
is that this essay will benefit the church by assisting its ministers and teachers to account for creation by our triune God for his glory and the good of
many others.

May our meditations upon Trinity and creation be blessed by God,
the Father, Son, and Holy Spirit, "for the manifestation of the glory of His
eternal power, wisdom, and goodness." May the Lord bless this work for the
good of all its readers and those who are served by them. Amen.

Appendix

The Majesty of Mystery:
Celebrating the Glory of an Incomprehensible God,
A Review Article

Cameron G. Porter[1]

THE MODERN THEOLOGICAL LANDSCAPE is such that most people in the pews, and many preachers in their pulpits, could not articulate what divine incomprehensibility is, nor could they comment on the historical significance of the doctrine.[2] Nevertheless, it is a doctrine necessary to teach, preach, and uphold. A presupposition at the outset of theological inquiry, divine incomprehensibility is grounded in God's own self-revelation in the Holy Scriptures, and confessed by the church throughout her history. Confessing God as incomprehensible is not to concede he cannot be *known*. God can be known; in fact, he has revealed himself unto that end. The confession rather is that God cannot be *comprehended*—he cannot be circumscribed within the confines of human contemplation. The positive affirmation of and proper approach to this essential component of theology keeps us on an orthodox path, preventing us from wandering into the forests of error on either side. Epistemic humility is the posture of the orthodox.

1 Cameron G. Porter is a member of Free Grace Baptist Church, Chilliwack, BC. This review article first appeared in *Journal of the Institute of Reformed Baptist Studies* (2017): 83–99 and is used with permission though some revisions were added.

2. The doctrine served the patristics well in combating the Christological heresies of the first six centuries of the church, and served the Reformed well in opposing the Socinians and anti-Trinitarians of the seventeenth century.

THESIS AND GENERAL OVERVIEW OF THE BOOK

In *The Majesty of Mystery: Celebrating the Glory of an Incomprehensible God*,[3] author K. Scott Oliphint endeavors to spell out what divine mystery is in Scripture, what we are to believe regarding it, and how Christians are to worshipfully respond in light of it. Employing Romans 11:33–36 as a *locus classicus*, he presents the subject matter reasonably well in the first two chapters, acknowledging the priority of divine incomprehensibility in the order of theological discovery (4), highlighting the link between incomprehensibility and doxology (4–5), and dealing with two excesses associated with mystery—rationalism (6) and mysticism (8). Oliphint suggests a proper balance to these, noting divine mystery recognizes God's loftiness in contradistinction to our lowliness, and that it does not militate against the Christian responsibility—truly the joy—to understand and know God.

In chapter 3, "The Mystery of the Three-in-One," however, Oliphint begins to drift into what appears to be the purpose of the book: setting his covenantal properties thesis[4] within the larger *locus* of divine mystery, and using mystery as the medium to propose his theological agenda. In the course of his proposals, he not only packages his arguments within the wrappings of mystery but, ironically, unravels divine mystery in attempts to uphold it. The scope of this review article will not be to analyze each chapter, providing counterarguments for every element of Oliphint's presentation that is deemed objectionable. Instead, focusing on chapters 3 through 5, I will offer a critical assessment of Oliphint's approach to the mystery of divine condescension, and how he presents the doctrines of the Trinity and the incarnation of Jesus Christ in light of this.

The question governing Oliphint's discourse for the chapters in question is: "How can the Infinite One relate to finite creatures?" (95). The resolution provided by him is the cause of our present concern: God's "covenantal condescension" (102). In the third chapter Oliphint begins to lay the groundwork for this, his principle interest, writing "there are truths about the Trinity that pertain to creation (and redemption) that do not pertain to the Trinity, in and of itself" and "we confess the Triune God *as God*, and . . . the Triune God *as related to, and involved in, creation*" (47, italics original).

---

3. K. Scott Oliphint, *The Majesty of Mystery: Celebrating the Glory of an Incomprehensible God* (Bellingham, WA: Lexham Press, 2016).

4. In *God with Us: Divine Condescension and the Attributes of God* (Wheaton, IL: Crossway, 2012), Oliphint proposes that God "takes on characteristics that determine just how he will interact with us, and with creation generally" (12). For a good critique of Oliphint's thesis see James E. Dolezal, *All that is in God: Evangelical Theology and the Challenge of Classical Christian Theism* (Grand Rapids: Reformation Heritage Books; 2017), 91–97.

Using conventional language of "ontological" and "economic," and seeking to distance himself from charges of presenting "two trinities" (48), Oliphint suggests that the expressions of God in creation are "not [the] expression[s] of the ontological Trinity" (48) but newly acquired and expressed attributes or characteristics of the economic Trinity that the ontological Trinity prior to creation had "no need or occasion for" (48–49). Though repeatedly disclaiming that he is positing mutability in God, no amount of qualification can dismiss the charges that Oliphint's conception of the economic Trinity ascribes new things to God. For Oliphint, though remaining what he always was, God begins-to-be that which he was not before. Maintaining his eternal mode of existence, he unchangingly takes on what can only be deemed a temporal mode of existence in the execution of the economy. Oliphint believes it enough to maintain an immutability where the ontological Trinity does not *change into* the economic Trinity so as to lose anything of what he is prior to creation. God "in Himself" (49) does not change, but God "in creation" (49) has occasion to express himself in new ways because of his interaction "in and with His creation" (49). This language of Oliphint should strike the attentive reader as presenting a problem. If the ontological Trinity needs to take on a particular existing state by which he can engage with his creation, then his creatures are not in relationship with the *eternal God* but with a *temporal version of that God* marked by new and extraneous properties. Besides presenting a dilemma for Christian worship,[5] this is not the classical view of divine immutability intended when our forebears, with the propriety and sanction of the Scriptures, echoed "in Him there is no Change."[6] All that God is, he is *essentially*—"the Begetter may not undergo change . . . He may not be God first and God last, nor receive any accession."[7]

This distinction by Oliphint is further developed in chapter 5, "The Majesty of the Mystery of God's Relationship to His People." After only setting the stage in previous chapters, Oliphint arrives at the terminus to which those other chapters tend—God's covenantal condescension whereby he takes to himself temporary and permanent characteristics in order to be

5. For an examination of the serious implications for worship in light of Oliphint's "covenantal properties" thesis, see James Dolezal, "Objections to K. Scott Oliphint's Covenantal Properties Thesis," Reformation21, July 2014, http://www.reformation21.org/articles/objections-to-k-scott-oliphints-covenantal-properties-thesis.php. Accessed 21 August 2015.

6. Augustine, *De Trinitate*, in NPNF, First Series, vol. 3, ed. Philip Schaff and Henry Wace (1894; reprint, Peabody MA: Hendrickson Publishers, 2012), 5.16.17. Taking their cues from the truths contained in passages such as Num. 23:19, Mal. 3:6, Heb. 6:17–18, and James 1:17, orthodox theologians have consistently upheld an essential, ontological immutability.

7. John of Damascus, *An Exposition of the Orthodox Faith*, NPNF2-09, I.8.

in relationship with us (105). Labeling this condescension "the model of majestic mystery" (75, 102), Oliphint distinguishes between "essential" and "covenantal" characteristics (102).[8] The former are those God has "whether or not there is creation . . . without which God would not be God," and the latter are those God has because of "creation, and the entrance of sin." The former are "primary" characteristics that "God has and is," "as God"; the latter are "secondary" characteristics that God has "as he relates himself to us" (101).[9] This should also strike the attentive reader as presenting a problem. If a distinguishing mark of the essential characteristics are that God has and is them *as God*, then *as whom* does he have the covenantal characteristics? If not *as God*, then it must be *as creature*. If, however, he has these characteristics *as divine* then was there lack in God *as God* prior to the acquisition of these characteristics? Or can he incur addition? If we accept Oliphint's "model of majestic mystery," we are forced by necessity to confess that God can be, in some way, augmented or made better. However freely he may decree and actualize this ontological newness, if God *as God* does not change into but instead, by the acquisition of properties, *becomes* God *in relation* (which is still change), Oliphint is faced with a timeless quandary. Either the new reality is

> for the better or for the worse. If for the better, then he must not have been infinite in perfection prior to the change, and therefore was not God. If for the worse, then he would no longer be infinite in perfection after the change, and therefore no longer God.[10]

Oliphint would do well to resolve with Ambrose: "nothing can be added to Him, and that alone which is Divine hath He in His nature."[11]

These retooled ontological-economic and absolute-relative distinctions are given Christological precedent in chapter 4, "The Majesty of the Mystery of the Incarnation." In this chapter, Oliphint employs the incarnation as a theological lodestar *par excellence* for understanding divine condescension. Labelling it the "substance" (205) and "climax of covenantal condescension" (76), Oliphint proposes that in the incarnation there is a

8. Also referred to as "absolute" and "relative" (101).

9. God does not relate himself to us; rather, God relates creatures to himself, either by nature or by grace (or both, in the case of the elect).

10. Stephen Charnock, *The Existence and Attributes of God*, two volumes (reprint, from the 1853 edition by Robert Carter & Brothers; Grand Rapids: Baker Book House Company, 1979, Eighth printing, February 1988), 1:331. Charnock was not the first, nor was he the last, to employ this biblically informed formula.

11. Ambrose, *Exposition of the Christian Faith*, NPNF, Second Series, vol. 10, ed. Philip Schaff and Henry Wace (1894; reprint, Peabody MA: Hendrickson Publishers, 2012), I.16.106.

"biblical distinction that is crucial to recognize, as it informs the way we must think about all of these biblical mysteries" (72). The stated distinction is the union of the two natures—divine and human—in the one person of Christ. Oliphint employs this distinction in order to draw parallels between it and the ontological-economic, absolute-relative distinctions that bookend this chapter. The doctrine of the incarnation is for him "an explanatory key"[12] to understand how *God transcendent* can also be *God condescended*. The argument goes like this: just as the Son of God freely took to himself human nature in the incarnation, so too has the triune God since creation freely taken to himself certain properties in order to relate to his creation. In asserting the liberty by which the Son assumes humanity and for the express purpose of equating it with the voluntary condescension of God in essence *becoming also* God in economy, Oliphint writes:

> There are significant and important differences, then, between the two natures in Christ. What is central in the incarnation is not the two natures, but the *Person*. It is the Person of the Son, even while He remained fully and completely the Son of God, who took to Himself a human nature in order to accomplish the salvation that we could not accomplish. The divine "nature" of the Son of God, therefore, is essential to who He is; the "nature" of man is who He is only because He freely decided He would take it. (73)

For Oliphint, the one person of Christ is to the divine and human natures as the one God is to the divine nature and acquired covenantal characteristics. Or, put another way, God-in-relation is God-in-himself plus acquired characteristics in order to relate, just as Christ in the unity of his Person is "very God and very Man, yet one Christ" (2LCF 8.2) in order to redeem. The reader is encouraged to inquire whether or not this sort of formula has ever been put forward in the history of the church, prior to our modern theological climate. Oliphint's proposal, inescapably, suggests that new things were added to God either essentially or according to some existential acquisition distinct from the divine nature. Isn't it mysterious? Though God is unchangeable, he changes. Though he is simple, he is composed. Though he is independent, he relies upon himself for decreed actuality. Though he is eternal, he endures succession in relation.

In the service of this construct, Oliphint bridges the gap between Old Testament theophanies and the incarnation when he writes that "the Son of God had been appearing to the saints throughout redemptive history

---

12. See James E. Dolezal, "Eternal Creator of Time," *Journal of the Institute of Reformed Baptist Studies* (2015): 138.

... by temporarily taking on various qualities and characteristics in order to be with his people" (74). Theophanies are, for Oliphint, not only God manifesting himself, or a revealing of the Son of God, but also and primarily instances of the Son assuming non-essential characteristics in order to reveal and to establish relational correspondence with his people. Similar to the permanent acquisition of characteristics that he keeps for eternity, the acquired temporary properties provide the existential parameters for God to properly relate to his people. This tends to inordinately maximize the nature of theophanies while simultaneously minimizing both the mode and uniqueness of the incarnation. This becomes most apparent when Oliphint writes that the Son of God

> never *permanently* took on a human nature until the point of His conception. This helps us recognize both the continuities and the discontinuities of the incarnation throughout redemptive history. One of the continuities is in the truth that the Son had been condescending really and truly, but temporarily and partially, in types and shadows all throughout covenant history. One of the discontinuities is that the incarnation was a *complete* and *perpetual* addition of a human nature to the Son. It was the climax to which the rest of covenant history had been pointing to all along. (74–75; italics original)

Unless there needed to be some editorial corrections to the way in which that was written, Oliphint asserts that the incarnation of the Son of God was marked by an *addition* of human nature to his divine person. His use of the word "addition" here is no small error. Throughout the history of the church's endeavor to defend orthodox Christology, the consistent emphasis of *union*[13] as the accepted incarnational terminology was frequently and deliberately set against *addition* in order to uphold the divine perfection of the Son.[14] Thomas Aquinas, echoing Cyril of Alexandria (one of his oft-cited theologians), upheld the hypostatic union by asserting:

> Since the Divine Person is infinite, no addition can be made to it: Hence Cyril says [Council of Ephesus, Part I, ch. 26]: "We do not conceive the mode of conjunction to be according to

13. Oliphint does employ the language of "took on a human nature" in the cited paragraph. This, along with "took to himself man's nature" has a rich pedigree in the history of orthodox Christology, and is language synonymous with *union*. However, such usage by Olipint is quickly undone by the use of *addition*, and is ultimately undone at large by his prevailing theology of "covenantal properties."

14. In the interest of protecting the doctrine of the person of Christ, modern homiletical platitudes such as "subtraction by addition," often employed in explaining the incarnation from Phil. 2:7, should be jettisoned from our Christological language.

addition"; just as in the union of man with God, nothing is added to God by the grace of adoption, but what is Divine is united to man; hence, not God but man is perfected.[15]

Four centuries later John Owen, for whom Aquinas was a theological progenitor, in a sermon concerning the "self-humiliation of the Son of God, in taking upon him our nature, for the discharge of the office of a mediator," faithfully articulated the same Christology when he preached:

> There is nothing can add unto God, unto his satisfaction. There is nothing wanting in himself unto his own eternal blessedness. . . There can be no addition made unto God. Therefore it must be an infinite condescension in him, and a humbling of himself, to behold the things done in heaven and on earth.[16]

Arthur W. Pink, consistent with his predecessors wrote:

> It was not by adding manhood to Godhead that His personality was formed. The Trinity is eternal and unchangeable. A new person is not substituted for the second member of the Trinity; neither is a fourth added. The person of Christ is just the eternal Word, who in time, by the power of the Holy Spirit, through the instrument of the virgin's womb, took a human nature (not at that time a man, but the seed of Abraham) into personal union with Himself.[17]

Further to his *addition Christology*, Oliphint contends that the preincarnate theophanic manifestations of the Son of God were incomplete and temporary instances of what was complete and permanent in the incarnation. They were, it seems, prognostic dress-rehearsals for the main event. Rather than the incarnation being that exclusive and unrepeatable event "when the fullness of the time was come" (Gal. 4:4), Oliphint attaches to it a progressively unfolding character, suggesting that the incarnation is co-extensive with redemptive history—the temporary and anticipatory instances of the acquisition of properties on the part of the Son in pre-incarnational Christophanies prefiguring the permanent and climactic assumption of human nature in the incarnation. Though he qualifies the Christophanic assumptions as temporary and the incarnation as permanent, and while he gives the incarnation greater redemptive-historical significance than previous divine assumptions, Oliphint's assertion that "the Son of God had been assuming, temporarily, certain characteristics . . . ever since creation" (74)

---

15. *Summa Theologica*, 3.3.1.

16. Sermon, Phil. ii. 5–8. November 9, 1681.

17. *The Nature of God* (Chicago: Moody Bible Institute, 1975, 1999), 198.

justly incurs the charge of rendering the hypostatic union *a common thing*. However elevated in its quintessence it may be in the mind of Oliphint, if the assumption of human nature by the Son is in fact "another instance when God . . . assumes certain characteristics . . . in order to relate Himself to His creation and to us" (73), then the incarnation is no longer the "new and ineffable mystery"[18] confessed by the church catholic, but simply the greater anticipated stoop of previous divine condescensions.

REFORMULATIONS: A PRICE TOO HIGH TO PAY

We must conclude that the price of Oliphint's reformulations is higher than the truth can afford. First, while he does not explicitly engage in a defining statement, clearly for Oliphint the explanation of "economic Trinity" is found in that God takes on and "[expresses] himself in 'new' characteristics in order to relate" (101). This presents a challenge to God's greatness and omnipotence. Repeating a particular formula of "in order to" and "so that he could" when articulating his conception of divine condescension, Oliphint suggests there is a "problem . . . of the distance of God" which God needs to voluntarily overcome because it "constitutes a boundary between the being of God and the being of creation" (97). Whether necessitated or assumed freely (Oliphint affirms the latter), this amounts to God having another manner in which he exists—an acquired mode of being that affords him the ontological conditions by which he can interact with his creation. This approach to divine condescension constitutes a form of theistic voluntarism which suggests that God, unconstrained by anything outside himself, freely and sovereignly wills to condescend to a state of actuality where he can be affected by, and react in time to, his creation. Purporting to preserve his independence and sovereignty, while also assuming to provide a more acceptable accounting for the biblical predications of divine affections, the voluntarist approach makes God the subject of his own agency. As it is with the bulk of the proposals relevant to Olipihint's covenantal condescension thesis, this not only contradicts divine simplicity, eternity, and immutability, it also unravels the very independence and sovereignty that are claimed to be preserved.[19] Contrary to Oliphint's assertions, the answer to the question

18. Alexander of Alexandria, *Epistles on the Arian Heresy*, ANF, vol. 6, ed. Alexander Roberts and James Donaldson (1886; reprint, Peabody MA: Hendrickson Publishers, 2012), VI.

19. For extended discussion on voluntarist approaches within contemporary Calvinism, see Charles J. Rennie, "A Theology of the Doctrine of Divine Impassibility: (I) Impassibility and the Essence and Attributes of God," in *Confessing the Impassible God*, 290–304.

of how this transcendent God can be in true and relational immanence is not found in the taking on of ontological newness "in order to relate," but in the fact that God is able to relate *because of who he is ontologically* (without the need of intermediary actuality).[20] This resolution preserves mystery. The essential divine perfections, themselves identical to God—unchanging, eternal, and suffering no diminution nor addition—do not bar the way of God's relationality but are the very foundation and explanation of it.

Second, Oliphint's conception of the economic Trinity, or God "as he relates himself to us" (101), departs from the theology of the historical church and serves to unravel the very mystery he is seeking to uphold. One may conclude Oliphint is simply demonstrating a failure to understand how the orthodox have defined "economic Trinity," and articulated the distinction between *absolute* and *relative* attributes. While this may be the case on some level, Oliphint's proposals are not misinterpretations of what the historic church has confessed but *explicit rejections* of that confession in favor of doctrinal novelty. Oliphint concedes this himself when he writes, "we can consider, however, *another way* of thinking of God's character" (102). Some will unfortunately applaud his temerity, but the rest of us should be very concerned when Oliphint remarks that the traditional "interpretations of the character of God . . . lack biblical support" and provide "no satisfactory way of affirming what the Bible *clearly* teaches about God" (94). Plainly confessing a departure from classical Christian orthodoxy, Oliphint suggests "we have to find a better way to interpret biblical passages dealing with God and His relation to the world" (94) than what the church has historically confessed.[21] He assures his readers that "fortunately, there is a better way to think theologically about God and about God's revelation of Himself" (94), and then offers that better way in the form of "covenantal condescension." The traditional discourse regarding the economic Trinity, however, has never proceeded from a perceived modal impasse that God must freely overcome in order to be the absolute who relates. It has been the assertion of antiquity that in the revelation of the economic Trinity we have the infinite and transcendent God condescending to our finitude to *reveal himself* in ways that we might understand, and

20. See Herman Bavinck, *Reformed Dogmatics*, gen. ed. John Bolt, trans. John Vriend (Grand Rapids: Baker Academic, 2004), 2:158, hereafter *RD*.

21. The danger in Oliphint's statement cannot be overstressed. If this was said with respect to other vital *loci* of theology, would it not be scandalous? If a professor of systematic theology at a notable Reformed seminary suggested the traditional interpretations regarding justification by faith alone lack biblical support, or that we have to find better ways of interpreting the biblical passages that deal with the divine inspiration of the Scriptures, would we applaud him for his ingenuity? Why, then, are such professors congratulated for, and encouraged to continue publishing, their newfangled conceptions of the triune God?

we have "the exercise of divine will and power, resulting in definite *temporal effects* in conformity with and as the execution or enactment of the eternal *decretum*."[22] In other words, the emphasis is upon *revelatory condescension* and the unfolding of eternal divine act, not upon *ontological condescension* marked by the acquisition of new attributes in time.

Third, and related to the above, Oliphint takes exception to analogical predication and the Scripture's use of figural language. Citing orthodox theologians who "encourage us to contradict what Scripture, in fact, says" (94),[23] Oliphint criticizes Augustine's interpretative "misstep" (91–92) when the latter writes, elaborating upon God's revelatory stoop to our finite capacities: "[Scripture] has borrowed many things from the spiritual creature, whereby to signify that which indeed is not so, but must needs so be said: as, for instance, 'I the Lord thy God am a jealous God'; and, 'It repenteth me that I have made man.'"[24] Taking exception to Augustine's assertion that Scripture uses figural language in many places "to signify that which *indeed is not so*, but must needs so be said" (such as God being jealous and repenting),[25] Oliphint renders the criticism "in other words, when Scripture ascribes something 'creaturely' to God, it is not telling us what God is like; it is saying something that is not the case" (92).[26] He goes on to affirm that anger, jealousy, and grief are properly predicated of God, though condescended.[27] Interestingly, Oliphint leaves out the beginning of the Augustine

22. Richard A. Muller, *Dictionary of Latin and Greek Theological Terms: Drawn Principally from Protestant Scholastic Theology* (Grand Rapids: Baker Book House, 1985), 213; italics added.

23. In addition to Augustine, Oliphint criticizes Stephen Charnock and Herman Bavinck for similar treatments of divine revelation. The reader should take pause to consider Oliphint's claim that these men misstepped in their handling of the biblical language concerning God. He is not only contending against these three men, but three men representing the entire stream of theological thought through the first nineteen centuries of Christian orthodoxy. If these highly-regarded theologians are wrong, then the innumerable company of respected theologians throughout the history of the Christian tradition are wrong as well. Calling to mind the fact that Calvin, Perkins, Ames, Owen, Turretin, Gill and a myriad of others before and after held the same view as Augustine, Charnock, and Bavinck, basically places the entire consensus of the orthodox (and certainly the Reformed) tradition in opposition to Oliphint's proposal.

24. Augustine, *De Trinitate*, 1.1.2.

25. Augustine, *De Trinitate*, 1.1.2, emphasis added.

26. The veracity and integrity of divine revelation does not depend upon a univocal literalism inherent to the predications of God in Scripture, but upon the foundation and authority of the divine author who employs language appropriate to our finitude. See Samuel Renihan, *God without Passions: A Reader* (Palmdale, CA: RBAP, 2015), 22–23.

27. In what we can only hope is an oversight, Oliphint writes: "God does become angry . . . the Holy Spirit can be, and is, grieved. All of these characteristics are true of God, even into eternity!" (106). Let alone the fact that Oliphint properly predicates anger and

quotation which states Scripture uses words "taken from things corpo-real, as when it says, 'Hide me under the shadow of Thy wings.'"[28] Surely Oliphint does not believe that God temporarily or permanently assumed the intermediary properties of feathered appendages.[29] Why then does he criticize Augustine for saying God does not properly have jealousy and grief if Augustine is right to state that the divine possession of newly-formed wings "indeed is not so?" By what consistent rule of interpretation is it ac-ceptable to affirm improper predication at the point of anthropomorphism (perhaps ornithomorphism?), but demand proper predication for instances of anthropopathism? Oliphint is certainly familiar with the classical and Reformed pedigree of upholding God's revelatory condescension, that such self-predications as "I am a jealous God" are instances of God speaking by "such representations as may suit and assist the capacity of the creature."[30] Yet Oliphint, dissatisfied with the older ways of talking about God, has abandoned that hermeneutical heritage for an interpretational literalism (i.e., biblicism) informed by his theology of covenantal properties.

Fourth, and finally, his use of the incarnation to argue the propriety of new actuality in God diminishes the uniqueness and glory of the incarna-tion. Nowhere does the Bible apply the mode, the rules, or the principles of reasoning demanded by the revelation of the incarnation to anything besides the incarnation itself. There is no modal parallel between the hypo-static union and the divine life post-creation. Whether creation, providence, or redemption—nothing brings about a change in the one who is infinite, eternal, and unchangeable. "He is unchangeably the same eternal God."[31] The fact that in Christ "two whole, perfect, and distinct natures were insepa-rably joined together in one person, without conversion, composition, or confusion" (2LCF 8.2) does not constitute a modal archetype for previous

---

grief of God, it appears that Oliphint believes God is angry and grieved "into eternity."

28. Augustine, *De Trinitate*, 1.1.2.

29. Cyril of Jerusalem notes: "There have been many imaginations by many persons, and all have failed. Some have thought that God is . . . a man with wings, because of a true text ill understood, *Thou shalt hide me under the shadow of Thy wings* [Ps. 17:8]. . . . For whereas God's protecting power was conceived as wings, they failing to understand this sank down to the level of things human, and supposed that the Unsearchable exists in the likeness of man." NPNF2–07; *The Catechetical Lectures of St. Cyril*, Chapter 7, "On the Unity of God." No doubt he agrees with Cyril, but "a true text ill understood" applies to Oliphint's interpretation of jealousy and repentance predicated of God.

30. Charnock, *Existence and Attributes*, 1:188. Gregory of Nyssa represents the *phronema patrum* when he observes "the Holy Spirit, in delivering to us the Divine mysteries, imparts that instruction which transcends reason by such methods as we can receive." NPNF2–05; *Dogmatic Treatises, Against Eunomius*, 2.9.

31. Bavinck, *RD*, 2:429.

or subsequent divine condescension. It is only in the grammar of the incarnation that we can say the boundless one is bounded (and only, of course, according to the assumed humanity). And yet Oliphint wants to extend this logic beyond the incarnation and into the life of God.[32] Consider the implications for a moment. If God since creation has been assuming characteristics he does not have essentially, and if these covenantal characteristics find a modal precedent in the incarnation of the Son of God, then everything God is as God-in-relation he is *as creature.* Given his incarnational pattern for all divine condescension, and given the fact that he already admits that anger and grief are properly ascribed to God, for Oliphint the rules of predication connected to the hypostatic union can also be applied to the economic Trinity. This is ultimately Oliphint's majestic mystery, that apart from the incarnation the following affirmations can be simultaneously true, but in distinct ways[33]: God is atemporal and temporal, being and becoming, immense and spatial, incorporeal and corporeal, simple and compounded, immutable and mutable, impassible and passible, incomprehensible and circumscribable, interminable and measured, every way infinite and exaltedly finite, Creator and creature. This is to dress contradiction in the garb of mystery. Not only has it been the confession of the historic church that everything God is he is essentially (that is, his existence and attributes are identical to his essence, and to each other), but that only within the "unrepeatable uniqueness"[34] of the incarnation of the person of the Son of God (and the attendant rules of predication afforded by the hypostatic union) can the church confess

> What is this novel mystery? The judge is judged and is silent; the invisible is seen and is not confounded; the incomprehensible is grasped and is not indignant at it; the immeasurable is contained in a measure and makes no opposition; the impassible suffers and does not avenge its own injury; the immortal dies and complains not; the celestial is buried and bears it with an equal mind.[35]

32. See Stefan T. Lindblad, "Unity and Distinction—One God in Three Persons: Unity of Essence, Distinction of Persons, Implications for Life, A Review Article," *JIRBS* (2015): 162–63.

33. I.e., according to Oliphint's "God in Himself"/"God in creation" (49), or "essential"/"covenantal" (102) dichotomous construct. As a remedy to this, see Francis Turretin, *Institutes of Elenctic Theology,* 3 vols., ed. James T. Dennison, Jr., trans. George Musgrave Giger (Phillipsburg, NJ: P&R Publishing, 1992–97), 2.13.5, for a discussion concerning the rules of predication that are exclusively confined to the theology of the incarnation.

34. Fred Sanders, *The Triune God* (Grand Rapids: Zondervan, 2016), 224.

35. Alexander of Alexandria, *Epistles on the Arian Heresy,* ANF, vol. 6, VI.

As noted previously, Oliphint bolsters this Christological precedent for covenantal characteristics by an appeal to Old Testament theophanies, particularly those assumed to have the Son of God as the subject of divine manifestation. For Oliphint, both the pre-incarnational Christophanic episodes and the incarnation itself are instances of the Son of God "taking on various qualities and characteristics in order to be with his people" and "expressing who he is in [those] characteristics" ensuring that "such a relationship could take place" (73–74). What is the problem with his proposal? Though the prevailing and overzealous all-theophany-is-Christophany approach to modern Christologies may need to consult Augustine,[36] we should certainly affirm the eternal existence and the revelation of the Son of God prior to his coming in the flesh. And though it may be too much for Oliphint to assert a frequency of appearances "to the saints" (74) on the part of the pre-incarnate Son, we certainly confess that the second person of the Trinity appeared to the prophets of the Old Testament.[37] The problem with Oliphint's theophany-incarnation construct is the assertion of a modal similarity between theophanic manifestations and the incarnation, and the description of the incarnation as "the Son of God permanently [taking] to himself characteristics that are not 'originally' His" (105).[38] It seems that, for Oliphint, just as in the incarnation

36. See Sanders, *The Triune God*, 224–26. Sanders helpfully cites Augustine in arguing for a more balanced approach to Old Testament theophanies, specifically rejecting the strong Christophanic emphasis in much of modern Christian thought. Noting the primary matter at hand is the "unrepeatable uniqueness of the incarnation of the Son," Sanders concludes that this more balanced non-Christophanic approach does not "deny that God is active in the Old Testament or in creation at large," but rejects the "notion that before or apart from the incarnation, the second person of the Trinity was the subject of visible mission." In the interest of protecting a robust, biblical trinitarianism and a high Christology, Augustine and many after him appealed to (a) the consubstantiality, and hence full equality, of the Son with the Father (and the Spirit); (b) from the doctrine of substantial unity the fact that all the divine works *ad extra* are the undivided works of the one true God—Father, Son, and Holy Spirit; and (c) the uniqueness of the sending of the Son in the incarnation.

37. John Owen reflects a balanced approach to the mystery when he writes: "I take it at present for granted that the Son of God appeared unto the prophets under the old testament. Whether ever he spake unto them immediately, or only by the ministry of angels, is not so certain." John Owen, *The Works of John Owen*, 23 vols. (Edinburgh; Carlisle, PA: The Banner of Truth Trust, 1965–1991), 19:21.

38. Confessionally speaking, it is judicious to write of "essential properties and common infirmities" (2LCF 8.2) in our articulations of the incarnation. This clause, however, does not stand on its own but follows "the Son of God . . . did . . . take upon him man's nature." Though Oliphint employs language consistent with this governing clause, his formula of "taking on various . . . characteristics" carries the predominance of repetition in his treatment. This appears to be deliberate, as it serves the larger proposal of a modal pattern in covenantal condescension.

there is a mode of conjunction[39] found in the assumption of humanity on the part of the Son, so must there be in the theophanic manifestations of the second person of the Trinity a mode of conjunction, of some sort (i.e., apposition, or accidental assumption), between his divine nature and the secondary characteristics accrued in covenantal condescension. Though he speaks to the consistencies and inconsistencies between them, there is not enough separation and distinction between the nature of theophany and the nature of the incarnation.[40] A modal parity is in fact granted to both, and the latter is diminished in the overestimation of the former.

In protecting what the Bible depicts as "reserving all pre-eminence"[41] for that occasion when the Son of God in "the fullness of the time" (Gal. 4:4) took to himself man's nature, we must remark that the difference between theophany and the incarnation is not simply a durational one, the former being transient and the latter permanent. Neither is the difference simply a chronological one, the former taking place in times past and the latter taking place in these last days. Nor is the difference between them only a

39. The language of "conjunction" is used deliberately here to highlight a measure of similarity Oliphint's language of the incarnation has with concepts and terminology objected to by the patristics and the latter scholastics in Christological controversies. In articulating a one-subject Christology in opposition to *tertium quid* and two-subject accounts of the incarnate Word, "union" was preferred over "conjunction" since the latter tended to a conception of apposition, or an accidental addition of humanity to divinity. Again, Thomas Aquinas resolved rightly "since the Divine Person is infinite, no addition can be made to it" (*Summa Theologica*, 3.3.1). In conflating the modality of theophany (as well as the permanent aspects of his covenantal condescension proposal) and incarnation into a model of "taking on various qualities and characteristics" (73), Oliphint is closer to an incarnational Christology of addition than he is to one of substantial or natural union. In fact, as noted previously, Oliphint explicitly employs the word "addition" in his Christological presentation when he writes: "the incarnation was a *complete* and *perpetual* addition of a human nature to the Son" [italics original].

40. Related to this, Oliphint's approach to the typology of theophany introduces another problem that diminishes the uniqueness of the incarnation. Certainly we confess that since the fall Christ and his redemptive benefits were revealed "in and by those promises, types, and sacrifices," him being "signified to be the seed which should bruise the serpent's head; and the Lamb slain from the foundation of the world" (2LCF 8.6). However, this confession is not characterized by a modal similarity between theophany and incarnation, nor that they both entail the same subject acquiring new characteristics. A type is not its anti-type; a shadow is not the substance that casts it; a sign is not the thing signified; a copy is not both the semblance and the reality of the true.

41. John Owen, *Works*, 19:17. There is much import to be brought to this discussion from the Epistle to the Hebrews. In asserting the surpassing excellence of Christ over all the articles of old covenant religion, and the perfection of the atoning work of the incarnate Son of God, the emphasis of the apostle is not upon the similarities but upon the attendant differences marking the first advent of Christ compared to those things that preceded and foresignified his coming.

qualitative one, as if to suggest that the incarnation is of the greatest magnitude among a class of divine condescensions. Nor is the difference between them only telic in nature, the former being anticipatory appearances that tended towards the consummative goal of the latter. Nor is the difference only with respect to the manner of revelation marking them, the former being delivered in sundry times and in divers manners and the latter coming immediately in and by the person of the incarnate Son of God. But the difference between theophanies and the incarnation is also a modal one—the former being a *mode of revelation*, and the latter marked uniquely[42] by a *mode of union* whereby the only-Begotten Son of God condescends to assume man's nature for our recovery. Contrary to Oliphint's assertions, theophanic manifestations are not instances of God condescending by the assumption of new characteristics unto a temporary mode of existence in order to relate to his people, and the incarnation is not a permanent instance of such assumption.[43] Simply put, the nature of the special divine presence in theophany is not the same as, but rather markedly different from, the nature of the incarnation of the Son.

Whether the proposal that God assumes permanent characteristics or temporary ones, the testimony of the Scriptures to the nature of God on the one hand, and the uniqueness of the incarnation on the other, will not afford such conceptions. The price is too high. If God has since creation been condescending to assume certain non-essential properties, and if these were in their manner either temporary or permanent anticipatory instances of what would be accomplished in the first advent of the Son, then the matchless marvel and mystery of the incarnation is just an exalted "well, *naturally.*" Given Oliphint's assertions, these ancient words ring fitting and true: "the wonder of the doctrine disappears, and there is nothing marvelous in what is alleged."[44]

---

42. The incarnation is also a manner of divine revelation (e.g., Heb. 1:1–2), but the emphasis here falls on the fact that theophanies were in no way instances whereby the Son took upon himself human (or angelic) nature, whether temporarily or permanently. The terminative act or work of the Son in assumption and unition is particular and exclusive to the incarnation.

43. Another important observation is that theophany is not the divine instrumentality required to bring the transcendent God near unto those blessed with the appearing. The transcendence of immensity is not set against the immanence of divine presence but entails and guarantees it, requiring no intermediary agency to actualize the nearness. While theophany is a special mode of the divine presence, this is simply according to the manner of a *revelatory*, not an *ontological*, condescension. Being repletively unbounded in his immensity, filling the heavens and the earth, God need not make himself to be circumscribed or definitively located in order to relate his creatures to himself.

44. Gregory of Nyssa, *Against Eunomius*, NPNF2–05, 6.3.1.

CONCLUSION

No doubt Oliphint has noble intentions in articulating his conceptions of divine condescension. As Reformed Christians with the same theological pedigree as Oliphint, we too love those sweet-sounding words of our Christian vocabulary[45]—"covenant," "condescension," "relationship"; we revel in those indispensable truths of our confession—the blessed Trinity, the incarnation, and the fact that God has stooped to reveal himself to the sons of men. We take no delight, then, in having to object to Oliphint's proposals in *The Majesty of Mystery* because Christians everywhere should *celebrate the glory of the incomprehensible God*. Yet perhaps having not completely considered the implications of his new theology, Oliphint has unraveled mystery in attempts to uphold it. "Wandering from the path of primitive doctrine, [he has] rushed into . . . error."[46] Though he asserts that objectors to his theology have engaged in "rationalizations that do an injustice to mystery as the lifeblood of theology" (106), when he answers the question of how God transcendent can be God condescended by suggesting the divine acquisition of new characteristics, mystery has given way to novelty.[47] Classical Christian orthodoxy has been content to acquiesce in mystery—worshipping the unchanging God who dwells in unapproachable light, resting in the confession that the one who made all things can relate all things to himself without having to become one of those things. Their treatments of the divine attributes and the condescension of God reflects this posture. In a book about the majesty of mystery, Oliphint should have been content to likewise acquiesce and resolve that "it is better to be ignorant without crime than to search with peril."[48] Bavinck, reflecting catholicity, is correct when he notes: "It is a mark of God's greatness that he can condescend to the level of his creatures and that, though transcendent . . . and, while absolutely maintaining his immutability, he can enter into an infinite number of relations to his creatures."[49] God is transcendent and immanent after all—but according to the heritage of antiquity and not the claims of the newfangled novelty.[50]

45. Paraphrase of the words of Rev. James McCann in *The Champion of Faith Against Current Infidelity* (London, UK: Wade & Co., 1882), Vol. 2 No.49, March 22, 1983.

46. Boethius, *The Theological Tractates*, V.5.

47. In Oliphint, *God with Us*, 43, he says, "In chapter 2, I will begin to outline a way of thinking about God's voluntary condescension. This chapter will begin to introduce a relatively new approach to a discussion of God's character."

48. Turretin, *Institutes*, 1.7.6.5.

49. Bavinck, *RD*, 2:159.

50. This is a paraphrase of Basil, *De Spiritu Sanctu*, NPNF2–08, 7.16.

Bibliography

BOOKS

à Brakel, Wilhelmus. *The Christian's Reasonable Service*, Volume I. Grand Rapids: Reformation Heritage Books, 1992, Third printing 1999.

Allen, Michael, and Scott R. Swain. *Christian Dogmatics: Reformed Theology for the Church Catholic*. Grand Rapids: Baker Academic, 2016.

―――. *Reformed Catholicity: The Promise of Retrieval for Theology and Biblical Interpretation*. Grand Rapids: Baker Academic, 2015.

Ames, William. *The Marrow of Theology*. Translated by John Dykstra Eusden. 1968; reprint, Grand Rapids: Baker Books, 1997.

Baines, Ronald S., Richard C. Barcellos, and James P. Butler, editors. *By Common Confession: Essays in Honor of James M. Renihan*. Palmdale, CA: RBAP, 2015.

Barcellos, Richard C. *The Family Tree of Reformed Biblical Theology: Geerhardus Vos and John Owen—Their Methods of and Contributions to the Articulation of Redemptive History*. Owensboro, KY: RBAP, 2010.

Barcellos, Richard C., editor. *Southern California Reformed Baptist Pastors' Conference Papers*. Volume I (2012). Palmdale, CA: RBAP, 2012.

Bavinck, Herman. *Reformed Dogmatics*. General editor John Bolt. Translated by John Vriend. Grand Rapids: Baker Academic, 2004.

Berkhof, Louis. *Systematic Theology*. 1939, 1941; reprint, Grand Rapids: Wm. B. Eerdmans Publishing Co., 1986.

Blowers, Paul M. *Drama of the Divine Economy: Creator and Creation in Early Christian Theology and Piety*. Oxford, UK: Oxford University Press, 2012.

Carson, D. A. *How Long, O Lord?: Reflections on Suffering and Evil*. Grand Rapids: Baker Publishing Group, 2006.

―――. *The Difficult Doctrine of the Love of God*. Wheaton, IL: Crossway Books, 2000.

Carter, Craig A. *Interpreting Scripture with the Great Tradition: Recovering the Genius of Premodern Exegesis*. Grand Rapids, MI: Baker Academic, 2018.

Charnock, Stephen. *The Existence and Attributes of God*. Two volumes. Reprint, from the 1853 edition by Robert Carter & Brothers. Grand Rapids: Baker Book House Company, 1979, Eighth printing, February 1988.

Cheynell, Francis. *The Divine Trinunity of the Father, Son, and Holy Spirit*. London: Printed by T. R. and E. M. for Samuel Gellibrand at the Ball in Pauls Church yard, 1650.

Coxe, Nehemiah. *Vindiciae Veritatis, or a Confutation of the heresies and gross errours asserted by Thomas Collier in his additional word to his Body of Divinity.* London: for Nathaniel Ponder, 1677.

Dennison, Jr., James T. *Reformed Confessions of the 16th and 17th Centuries in English Translation.* Volume 1, 1523–1552. Grand Rapids: Reformation Heritage Books, 2008.

———. *Reformed Confessions of the 16th and 17th Centuries in English Translation.* Volume 2, 1552–1566. Grand Rapids: Reformation Heritage Books, 2010.

———. *Reformed Confessions of the 16th and 17th Centuries in English Translation.* Volume 3, 1567–1599. Grand Rapids: Reformation Heritage Books, 2012.

———. *Reformed Confessions of the 16th and 17th Centuries in English Translation.* Volume 4, 1600–1693. Grand Rapids: Reformation Heritage Books, 2014.

Dolezal, James E. *All that is in God: Evangelical Theology and the Challenge of Classical Christian Theism.* Grand Rapids: Reformation Heritage Books, 2017.

Duby, Steven J. *Divine Simplicity: A Dogmatic Account.* London, New York, Oxford, New Delhi, Sydney: T&T Clark, 2016.

———. *God in Himself: Scripture, Metaphysics, and the Task of Christian Theology.* Downers Grove, IL: IVP Academic, 2019.

Emery, Gilles. *The Trinitarian Theology of St. Thomas Aquinas.* Oxford; New York: Oxford University Press, 2007.

———. *The Trinity: An Introduction to Catholic Doctrine on the Triune God.* Washington, D.C.: The Catholic University of America Press, 2011.

Fesko, J. V. *The Spirit of the Age: The 19th-Century Debate over the Holy Spirit and the Westminster Confession.* Grand Rapids: Reformation Heritage Books, 2017.

Feser, Edward. *Scholastic Metaphysics: A Contemporary Introduction.* Piscataway, NJ: Translation Books Rutgers University, 2014.

Frame, John M. *Salvation belongs to the Lord: An Introduction to Systematic Theology.* Phillipsburg, NJ: P&R Publishing, 2006.

———. *Systematic Theology: An Introduction to Christian Belief.* Phillipsburg, NJ: P&R Publishing, 2013.

———. *The Doctrine of God.* Phillipsburg, NJ: P&R Publishing, 2002.

Gill, John. *A Body of Doctrinal and Practical Divinity.* Paris AR: The Baptist Standard Bearer, 1989.

Hodge, Charles. *Romans.* Reprint 1989; Edinburgh and Carlisle, PA: The Banner of Truth Trust, 1835.

Horton, Michael. *Rediscovering the Holy Spirit: God's Perfecting Presence in Creation, Redemption, and Everyday Life.* Grand Rapids: Zondervan, 2017.

Junius, Franciscus. *A Treatise on True Theology.* Translated by David C. Noe. Grand Rapids: Reformation Heritage Books, 2014.

Kelly, Douglas F. *Creation and Change: Genesis 1.1–2.4 in the Light of Changing Scientific Paradigms.* Geanies House, Fearn, Ross-shire, Scotland, UK: Mentor, 1997, re. 2010.

Levering, Matthew. *Engaging the Doctrine of Creation: Cosmos, Creatures, and the Wise and Good Creator.* Grand Rapids: Baker Academic, 2017.

Lillback, Peter A., ed. *Seeing Christ in all of Scripture: Hermeneutics at Westminster Theological Seminary.* Philadelphia, PA: Westminster Seminary Press, 2016.

Manton, Thomas. *An Exposition of the Epistle of James.* Grand Rapids: Associated Publishers and Authors Inc., n.d..

Mascall, E. L. *He Who Is: A Study in Traditional Theism*. London, New York, Toronto: Longmans, Green and Co., 1943.

McFarland, Ian A. *From Nothing: A Theology of Creation*. Louisville: Westminster John Knox Press, 2014.

McGraw, Ryan M. *Knowing the Trinity: Practical Thoughts for Daily Life*. Lancaster, PA: Alliance of Confessing Evangelicals, 2017.

Muller, Richard A. *Dictionary of Latin and Greek Theological Terms*. Second Edition. Grand Rapids: Baker Academic, 1985, 2017.

———. *Post-Reformation Reformed Dogmatics: The Rise and Development of Reformed Orthodoxy, ca. 1520 to ca. 1725, Volume Four, The Triunity of God*. Grand Rapids: Baker Academic, 2003.

Muller, Richard A. and Rowland S. Ward. *Scripture and Worship: Biblical Interpretation and the Directory for Public Worship*. The Westminster Assembly and the Reformed Faith, vol. 1. Edited by Carl R. Trueman. Phillipsburg, NJ: P&R Publishing, 2007.

Oliphint, K. Scott. *Covenantal Apologetics: Principles & Practice in Defense of Our Faith*. Phillipsburg, NJ: P&R Publishing, 2013.

———. *God with Us: Divine Condescension and the Attributes of God*. Wheaton, IL: Crossway, 2012.

———. *The Majesty of Mystery: Celebrating the Glory of an Incomprehensible God*. Bellingham, WA: Lexham Press, 2016.

Ortlund, Gavin. *Theological Retrieval for Evangelicals: Why We Need Our Past to Have a Future*. Wheaton, IL: Crossway, 2019.

Owen, John. *Biblical Theology or The Nature, Origin, Development, and Study of Theological Truth in Six Books*. Pittsburgh, PA: Soli Deo Gloria Publications, 1994.

———. *The Works of John Owen*. Volume 3. Edited by William H. Goold. Edinburgh: The Banner of Truth Trust, 1988 edition.

———. *The Works of John Owen*. Volume 12. Edited by William H. Goold. Edinburgh: The Banner of Truth Trust, 1982 edition.

———. *The Works of John Owen*. Volume 17. Edited by William H. Goold. Edinburgh: The Banner of Truth Trust, 1991 edition.

Perkins, William. *A Golden Chain, or The Description of Theology*. 1597; reprint, Puritan Reprints, 2010.

Poole, Matthew. *A Commentary on the Whole Bible, Volume I: Genesis–Job*. Edinburgh; Carlisle, PA: The Banner of Truth Trust, Reprinted 1974.

Renihan, James M. *A Toolkit for Confessions: Helps for the Study of English Puritan Confessions of Faith*. Palmdale, CA: RBAP, 2017.

Sanders, Fred. *The Deep Things of God: how the Trinity changes everything*. Wheaton, IL: Crossway, 2010.

———. *The Triune God*. New Studies in Dogmatics. Michael Allen and Scott R. Swain, general editors. Grand Rapids: Zondervan, 2016.

Treier, Daniel J. *Introducing Evangelical Theology*. Grand Rapids, MI: Baker Academic, 2019.

Turretin, Francis. *Institutes of Elenctic Theology*. 3 volumes. Edited by James T. Dennison, Jr. Translated by George Musgrave Giger. Phillipsburg, NJ: P&R Publishing, 1992–97.

Van Til, Cornelius. *Common Grace and the Gospel*. Second Edition. Edited by K. Scott Oliphint. Phillipsburg, NJ: P&R Publishing, 2015.

Vos, Geerhardus. *Biblical Theology: Old and New Testaments*. 1948; reprint, Grand Rapids: Wm. B. Eerdmans Publishing Company, June 1988.

————. *Reformed Dogmatics, Volume One: Theology Proper*. Translated and edited by Richard B. Gaffin, Jr. Bellingham, WA: Lexham Press, 2012–2014.

Ussher, James. *A Body of Divinity: Being the Sum and Substance of the Christian Religion*. 1648; reprint, Birmingham, AL: Solid Ground Christian Books, 2007.

Watson, Thomas. *A Body of Divinity: Contained in Sermons upon the Westminster Assembly's Catechism*. Edinburgh and Carlisle, PA: The Banner of Truth Trust, 2000.

Webster, John. *God without Measure: Working Papers in Christian Theology, Volume I, God and the Works of God*. London, Oxford, New York, New Delhi, Sydney: Bloomsbury, 2016.

Weinandy, Thomas G. *Does God Change? The Word's Becoming in the Incarnation*. Still River, MA: St. Bede's Publications, 1985.

Witsius, Herman. *Sacred Dissertations of the Apostle's Creed*. Volume 1. 1823; reprint, Grand Rapids, Reformation Heritage Books, 2010.

Wollebius, Johannes. "Compendium Theologiae Christianae." In *Reformed Dogmatics*. Edited and Translated by John W. Beardslee III. Grand Rapids: Baker Book House, 1977.

Wuellner, Bernard. *Dictionary of Scholastic Philosophy*. Fitzwilliam, NH: Loreto Publications, 2012.

ARTICLES

Dolezal, James E. "Eternal Creator of Time." *Journal of the Institute of Reformed Baptist Studies* (2014): 125–51.

McFarland, Ian F. "The Gift of the *Non aliud*: Creation from Nothing as a Metaphysics of Abundance," *International Journal of Systematic Theology*, Volume 21, Number 1, (January 2019): 44–58.

McGraw, Ryan M. "Toward a Biblical, Catholic, and Reformed Theology: An Assessment of John Frame's *Systematic Theology: An Introduction to Christian Belief*." *Puritan Reformed Journal*, 8, 2, (2016): 197–211.

Porter, Cameron G. "*The Majesty of Mystery: Celebrating the Glory of an Incomprehensible God*, A Review Article." *Journal of the Institute of Reformed Baptist Studies* (2017): 83–99.

INTERNET LINKS

Bucey, Camden. "Addressing the Essential-Covenantal Model of Theology Proper." Available at https://reformedforum.org/addressing-the-essential-covenantal-model-of-theology-proper/. Accessed 5 June 2019.

Dolezal, James E. "Objections to K. Scott Oliphint's Covenantal Properties Thesis." Available at http://www.reformation21.org/articles/objections-to-k-scott-oliphints-covenantal-properties-thesis.php. Accessed 5 January 2018.

Oliphint, K. Scott. "Aquinas: A Shaky Foundation." Available at https://www.thegospelcoalition.org/article/aquinas-a-shaky-foundation/. Accessed 4 November 2017.

————. "Theological Principles from Van Til's Common Grace and the Gospel." Lecture delivered at the 2014 Reformed Forum Theology Conference, Gray's Lake, IL, October 2014. Available at http://reformedforum.org/rf14_08/. Accessed 30 March 2015.

Waddington, Jeffrey C. "Something So Simple I Shouldn't Have to Say It." Available at https://reformedforum.org/something-so-simple-i-shouldnt-have-to-say-it/. Accessed 15 February 2020.

Weinandy, Thomas G., Thomas. "Human Suffering and the Impassibility of God." *Testamentum Imperium* Volume 2, 2009: 1–19. Available at http://www.precious heart.net/ti/2009/52-. Accessed 9 February 2015.

CPSIA information can be obtained
at www.ICGtesting.com
Printed in the USA
LVHW081401080822
725431LV00003B/146